The Psychology of

Mind Deception

The Fascinating World of

101 Cognitive Biases

ROBIN K. MATHEW

© Robin K Mathew 2023

Email ID: anahithamag@gmail.com

The Psychology of Mind Deception

Author:

Dr. Robin K Mathew is a seasoned psychologist and accomplished writer, and his journey unfolds as a tapestry woven with rich experiences and profound insights. With a career spanning the globe, Dr. Robin K Mathew has had the privilege of engaging with individuals from nearly 90 different nationalities, each representing a mosaic of socio-economic, ethnic, and linguistic backgrounds. He has academic qualifications and working experience in areas like Information Technology, Human Resource Management, Psychology, Cyber Forensics, and Cyber Psychology. He has worked in prestigious organizations like the University of Toronto, Best Buy, The Indian Institute of Management, ICFAI Business School, and the Royal Bank of Canada. This extensive exposure has crafted a diverse understanding of human behavior and life in its myriad forms. Over the past twelve years, his written work has found a home in several prestigious magazines, both in India and abroad. To date, he has authored close to 500 articles across a wide spectrum of subjects, infusing each piece with the wisdom and insight gained through this work. He has successfully authored and published 14 more books, each offering a unique exploration of diverse facets of human psychology and the human condition.

Other Books:
1. Madampalliyile Manorogikal (Malayalam)
2. The Expedition of a Nun (Novel)
3. Chekuthante Panipura (Malayalam)

Email:robinkmathew@gmail.com

Table of Contents

Introduction

The Psychology of Mind Deception

The Psychology of Mind Deception

Introduction

Are you really that smart? Is your brain too strong? Are you a logical thinker? Would you be able to recognize a piece of fake news? Do you easily realize that other people are cheating on you? Is our brain a truth-seeking machine?

If you answered yes to all of the above questions, then remember - all your assumptions are wrong. This book talks about how your mind plays tricks with you. This book illustrates 101 cognitive biases to explain how our brain is an illogical, pattern seeking machine.

What is a cognitive bias?

Cognitive biases can be translated as perceptual biases, intellectual biases. A cognitive bias is a systematic error in thinking that occurs when people interpret information from the world around them.

The human brain is powerful but subject to limitations. Cognitive biases are often the result of your brain's attempt to absorb information and process them rapidly. These biases often act as rules that help us make sense of the world and make decisions with relative speed.

Some of these biases are related to memory. The way you remember an event can be biased for several reasons. It can lead to biased thinking and error in decision- making. Other cognitive biases are related to problems with attention. Attention is a limited resource. People choose what they care about in the world around them. So subtle biases can influence the way you see and think about the world.

The concept of cognitive bias was first introduced in 1972 by researchers Amos Tversky and Daniel Kahneman. Since then, researchers have described various types of biases,that affect decision-making in various fields. Including social behavior, cognition, and behavioral economics. These concepts have an impact on every field including health care, business ,education, management and finance.

1. Availability Heuristic

Which transport is the most dangerous? A person traveling by road or traveling by air, which one is safer?

Approximately 1.3 million people die each year as a result of road traffic crashes. More than half of all road traffic deaths are among vulnerable road users: pedestrians, cyclists, and motorcyclists. If you take the number of airplane crashes, it varies yearly, but roughly, assume that there are between 70-90 crashes per year. Keep in mind that includes all types of crashes, including commercial planes and privately-owned ones worldwide. But after reading the news of a plane crash, you hesitate to travel by air. But you don't hesitate anyway to travel by car or two- wheeler. Because that's how important the media reports plane crashes.

Reports of child abductions, plane crashes, and train derailments often lead people to believe that such events are far more common than they are. For example, after watching a movie about a nuclear disaster, you start to worry about the possibility of a nuclear war or accident. After seeing a car overturned on the side of the road, you may believe that your car is more likely to be in an accident. The more that event lingers in your mind, the more it will affect your decisions. This is due to excessive media coverage. But sometimes the novelty or drama surrounding an event can make it stick in your memory more.

The Psychology of Mind Deception

When we have to make important decisions about the future, we use the information that comes to our minds quickly and easily. That means to make a decision we would not bother to rely on detailed statistics. This is called the availability heuristic. A heuristic is an intellectual shortcut. The availability heuristic can lead us to make bad decisions because the information that can be easily recalled is often insufficient to understand how likely important future events are to occur again. Ultimately, it provides the decision maker with low-quality information on which to base their decision.

Examples:

In politics, at the time of the election a leader comes and people vote for him with some trust. He comes to power and completes his tenure without fulfilling any promises. The next person comes and swears that he will fulfill the promises that the previous one did not keep. He also comes to power and returns without fulfilling his promises. It repeats. The bottom line is that people only remember what the candidates say when the election is approaching. You have a one- in- a million chance of winning the lottery. Especially American lotteries like Power Lotto. But why do so many people buy the lottery? The chances of you dying in an accident while going to buy the lottery are many times greater than the chances of winning the lottery. But when you see a piece of news that someone has won the lottery, you will be forced to buy a lottery ticket.

2. Affect Heuristic

When we make decisions we mainly rely on our emotions at the time. Even when taking important decisions we do not take into account any correct situational information. This emotionality can help us to reach a quick decision but it can affect our logic and lead to flawed decisions. The emotions that influence you while making decisions are called affect and the mental shortcut to reach that decision is called heuristic.

The affect heuristic accompanies every decision in life. When you're happy, you're more likely to take risks. But when you feel depressed, you don't embark on any significant endeavors. Your mind thinks that everything is more rewarding and less risky when you are happy. But when the mind is disturbed, you see only danger and possibility of failure.

For example, Priya is a girl who sings well. She gets an opportunity to participate in a leading Television channel reality show. But the day before going for the audition, she gets her school progress card. She has failed miserably in many subjects. Her confidence gets shattered. She decides not to go to the singing competition. Actually her failure in school exams had nothing to do with her singing ability. But the emotion of her failure at that moment leads her to a decision to throw away the best chance of her life.

The Psychology of Mind Deception

It is this emotion that often influences us when we are under significant pressure to make a quick decision. When we embark on a new venture, the first feeling that dominates us is an intuition that we will fail. This one emotion prevents us from stepping out of our comfort zone.

Research has shown that Americans are well aware of climate change, but do not consider it a serious problem. Many people report that they have not experienced the effects of climate change. They feel it is a long-term phenomenon and that it will not occur soon. Therefore, they also do not feel that something should be done to address global climate change. When a leader takes an emotional shortcut like this, it can have far-reaching effects on that community. Especially if that decision pertains to an organization, a city or a country,

The affect heuristic can often be used to bring about positive changes in society. When it comes to public health, fear can be used for good to persuade people to abandon unhealthy habits. It has been found that showing scary statistics about cancer and disfigured body parts caused by smoking in movie theaters helps to reduce smoking in society.

3. Affinity Bias

We have probably heard many stories of people who failed miserably in technical interviews but got the job because they played the same game as the manager or had the same interests as him.

Every person thinks that we are very good at understanding people's character. We would agree that an HR manager who interviews a lot of people is a great person to understand people. But we get suspicious when the person she interviewed and selected leaves the company and gets fired within a month. Most of the time we choose those who are compatible with our preferences, life circumstances, and beliefs. If you are a manager, you must have had the experience of having an all-around brilliant person come in for an interview and turn him down for the sole reason that the "chemistry" with him is not right.

Unconscious Perceptual Bias and Affinity Bias

Affinity bias is an unconscious process. There is a reason for that. Since thinking itself is an energy-consuming process, our brains have evolved to try to minimize it. About eleven million pieces of information enter our brains every second. It comes in the form of sound, light, smell, and experience. But our brain can handle only 40 pieces of information at a time. So we use some shortcuts to make decisions. When we meet new people, we judge them based on factors such as their gender, ethnicity, beauty, color, and religion. We often make these quick judgments unconsciously

This decision-making happens even before you know it. We judge a person by how they look, speak, dress, and present themselves. We judge him by comparing her personality traits that fall within our mental framework.

A manager often hires only those who fit within a cultural framework that she deems appropriate. Many brilliant people will be put off by this. In these companies, there will be a group of people with almost the same mindset. The possibility of coming up with new and diverse ideas is closed here.

4. Anchoring Bias

Why do we rely so much on the first information we receive? Anchoring bias is closely related to the process of decision making. An "anchor" is the information currently available to us when making a decision. The decisions we make later depend on this first information. This means that the first received information acts as an anchor in our mind.

For example, if you first see a T-shirt priced at Rs 1,000 and then see a second T-shirt priced at Rs 500, you are more likely to buy the second shirt. If the first shirt you see is Rs 120 and the second one is Rs 200, there are more chances for you to buy the first shirt. Here, the price of the first shirt is the criterion for your decision. An important part of anchoring bias is the tendency to use the first piece of information as an 'anchor'. This 'anchor' is the reference point for later future decisions, expectations, or judgments.

Used car dealers often use these 'anchors'. Instead of asking the customer for 3 lakhs for the car, the salesman asks for 5 lakhs. Negotiations take place. Finally the seller says he will sell the car for three and a half lakhs. Then another half lakh is deducted. Five lakhs is the anchor here. The seller gets the price he intended. And the customer feels they are getting a better deal. This means that all our calculations depend on the information we receive first.

We unconsciously use anchoring bias to make more rational decisions. However, in reality, it can have the opposite effect. We give too much importance to the first information we hear or receive. Remember that doing this is not based on any evidence or logic. Our mind thinks that these decisions based on the limited information are a rational decision. Even if some prior information is available before making a decision, this 'anchor' can often have a false influence on our decision.

a. Consensus negotiations

Research from Harvard University shows that negotiating to reach an agreement is a good example of anchoring bias. First-hand information can have a significant impact on negotiations. Often, the other party will wait for the first offer to be made. This will throughout influence further discussions.

b. In the courtroom

Often, we see judges awarding different sentences for almost identical crimes. This is related to anchoring bias. A previous judgment elsewhere in a similar case affects all subsequent judgments. The sentence recommended by prosecutors will also affect their verdict.

c. Marketing

This perceptual bias comes into play in marketing and advertising. This 'anchor' is an important tool for increasing sales. Big retail chains such as Wal-Mart frequently use large price increases and then offer discounts on frequently sold items of the same price.

5. Attention Bias

Do you consider all possibilities when making an important decision? We think we'll consider all the possibilities on such an occasion. But the truth is that we don't take into account many of the possibilities that we know about. We pay attention to very few things. And we ignore most of the things. This perceptual bias is called attentional bias.

Attention bias is a form of tunnel vision. It also has evolutionary properties. In any situation, we have learned to notice only the changes that we need (both good and bad) and ignore the majority of changes that occur around us. This gave us the ability to find food and remain less vulnerable to other animals. Anyone who's ever had to run from a fire or an intruder, or run to finish a big project when a deadline looms, knows the upside of tunnel vision.

There is a dark side to this tunnel vision. This is what psychologists often have to deal with. People with depression, anxiety disorders, etc see only the dark sides around them. Not only our mental state but also physical states create this attention bias . If you shop when you're hungry, you're more likely to buy more food. You forget your diet during that time and eat more high -calorie and sugary foods.

This attentional bias leads to irrational racial profiling and prejudice among police officers. Black people, especially young people, are often misrepresented as dangerous criminals. This bias causes it to judge people negatively. Of this perception, many think that black faces are implicitly linked to crime

6. Bandwagon Effect

The bandwagon effect refers to the perceptual bias in which the majority of people follow a particular way of doing or believing a specific thing. The bandwagon phenomenon refers to ideas that are attached to each other and travel long distances at high speeds, like the bogies of a train.

The more the number of people believes in something, the more and more people believe the same thing. The number of people who think away from this will soon dwindle. All human beings tend to conform to the prevailing beliefs and customs of society. Their reason has only second place. No one wants to be left out of the mainstream of society. Therefore, we are afraid to have an opinion that is different from the general public. Often, we are quick to believe and then accept the ideas or beliefs of the larger social group or 'majority' as correct. It is not something we do consciously. We will not consciously accept the majority's opinion. But our subconscious mind must have accepted that opinion. This is because, we always want to be on the 'winning side'. Going against the majority opinion is like trying to stem the tide and trying to swim against the current. And that is dangerous too.

The popularity of certain products makes more people jump on this train of choice. This is the social psychology of videos going viral. We love many brands because we get on the bandwagon of this majority opinion. For example, we would choose a brand of wine that quickly runs out of the store shelves. The seller also tells us that this is the best and that most people have bought it. In the world of fashion, we tend to use the brands that celebrities use the most.

Most people try to agree with what other people believe, avoiding the difficult process of analyzing something and coming to an opinion on their own. This bandwagon effect is very much present in politics. Even candidates who are 100% sure that they will lose the coming election will say that they will win. It is because humans tend to stick with the people who win. The same effect occurs among voters when Gallup poll results are released before an election. More and more people will flock in a wave of comments.

US invasion of Iraq

The American public was generally in favor of George Bush's completely reactionary decision to invade Iraq as it had chemical weapons stockpiles. When experts around the world generally disagreed with the decision to attack Saddam Hussein, what changed the American people's opinion?

It was a bandwagon effect created deliberately by the American media. The media was very efficient in presenting the arguments of the Bush administration to the people that there was no other way to save the world and the American people from terrorism than to attack Saddam Hussein. The American media has hidden from its people all the world's arguments and suggestions about non-war solutions to solve one problem. The fast-paced coverage of media such as CNN, MSNBC, and Fox News has prevented people from thinking about other ways to solve the problem and prevented them from analyzing the information in depth.

7. Barnum Effect / Forer Effect

The Forer effect is the tendency to think that sentences that apply to all individuals, in general, are accurate descriptions of oneself. It was discovered by psychologist Bertram R Forever.

Consider the following sentences about your personality:

"You want to be loved and respected by other people. You deliberately hide some flaws in your character from others. You often have the feeling that you have not reached a level according to your potential. You often have a feeling that your ability is not recognized enough.

Although you are a mentally disciplined person, at times you become impatient and behave as if you have lost your courage. Sometimes it seems that many decisions made in the past were not the right ones. Feelings that other people have often exerted undue influence on your life are bothering you now.

You are a free thinker. You do not take other people's words for granted. Even Though you are friendly to everyone, at times you turn out to be a bit of an introvert. Sometimes you feel that some of your decisions are so unrealistic."

As you read this, you must have felt that it was written about you.

This was copied from a weekly magazine. Dr. Forer gave this characterization to some college students in 1948. He asks the children to analyze how much the things mentioned in it agree with their character and give them zero to five marks according to their agreement.

Zero - not my personality traits at all.

Five - completely my character traits.

This experiment has since been performed over a thousand times by various psychologists at various universities. The average for this test is still 4.2 out of five. That means 84 percent of people say that it is their character traits.

There are hundreds of thousands of people in this world who live with wild cold reading like this. It is also a multi-billion dollar industry. If someone praises you, you will believe it. Your faith in the speaker will make you believe what he is saying.

This effect exists in many professions and industries. Companies like Netflix, Amazon, and Facebook seem to offer personalized features and personalized movie lists for each user. This gives consumers the illusion of a customized product. These technology companies are effectively using the Barnum effect to give their software users the illusion of a personalized product. They often just give everyone a list that the majority likes.

The Pollyanna principle

Another psychological phenomenon that explains the working principles of the Barnum effect / Forer effect is the theory of poly (positivity bias). This bias is the tendency of people to remember happy events more accurately than negative ones. It makes sense, right?

The Psychology of Mind Deception

Why would anyone want to remember things that make them unhappy or unpleasant? Basically we like to remember happy memories. The same is true of the Barnum effect. We prefer what we want to hear about ourselves.

8. Cashless Effect

Suppose you are going shopping at the store. If you have a credit card, debit card, or online payment system, you'll buy more and spend more than you would with cash.

For example, you walk into an electronics store. A new model cell phone is seen in the store. The chances of you paying Rs 25,000 cash to buy it are very low. First, the chances of keeping that much cash in hand are low. And it's not safe. Even if you have that amount in hand, your mind hesitates to take it and give it to someone. When you pay cash you feel like something is missing. But you can easily spend such a large amount on a credit card without any emotional difficulty.

In a study of two major US apartment complexes, researchers found that people spent less money on laundry when machines accepted coins than when using a prepaid card system. In short, paying by card forces apartment dwellers to spend more money on their laundry.

Researchers at MIT asked people to bid for a pair of tickets for a sporting event. One group was told that they could pay with a credit card, while the other group was told they had to pay in cash. It was found that people in the credit card group bid up to 72% more on tickets than those told to pay in cash.

Advantages of online payment:

1. Money is not stolen; Because there is no obvious money here

2. Less money laundering because a digital record is always left behind.

3. Time and cost savings associated with handling, storing, and depositing paper money

4. Easy currency exchange when traveling internationally.

Disadvantages:

1. Your personal information is disclosed with every payment transaction.

2. If hackers steal your bank account or you experience any technical issues, you will be left out with no other source of funds.

3. Those without bank accounts or mobile phones will struggle to adapt to cashless technology.

The Psychology of Mind Deception

4. Some may find it difficult to control spending when they do not see physical money being spent out of their hands.

9. Bike Shedding (law of trivialities)

The Law of Triviality refers to the fact that people in an organization spend a lot of time and energy on trivial and irrelevant things. A situation where the officials of a nuclear power plant are discussing more on where and how to park their bikes .In this due course they completely forget about discussing the technical or financial aspects of the nuclear power plant .This is an excellent example of bikeshedding.

Let's look at other examples. A company has appointed a committee to discuss three issues:

1. Construction of a large reactor.

2. Construction of a small bike shed.

3. Budget for coffee for the meeting.

Nuclear reactors are a complicated issue, and few of the committee members know much about the subject. When they are asked to discuss it, they talk about it for just two or three minutes. After that, they quickly agree on the subject and move on to the next item on the list. The next item is the construction of the bike shed. They start discussing it. Many members of this committee felt that they did not make a clear contribution to the meeting because they did not have anything to say on the first topic. So they waste time debating whether the roof of the bike shed should be made of aluminum or galvanized iron. Finally, 45 minutes later, after finding ways to save a small amount of money on the bike shed project, they end the discussion on the topic with a sense of accomplishment.

Then, they move on to the last item on the list. This item is the annual coffee budget for meetings. Many find that this topic is one of the most important things on their agenda and one of the easiest for them to understand. They discuss it fiercely.

There are many reasons why people focus on trivial matters while neglecting more important ones.

Common reasons for this include:

1. It is easy to understand simple problems and form an opinion.

2. It takes very little time, effort, money, or mental energy to solve a simple problem.

3. They will have to take more responsibility for their decisions if they focus on the main issue.

4. The rest assume that the key issues may have been assessed and resolved by those responsible.

The Psychology of Mind Deception

Bike Shedding at other locations

Do you remember teachers going off track with the curriculum while teaching in the classroom? They probably spent a large part of your biology class time telling you a personal story and avoiding important scientific theories. In such a case, your teacher was a victim of bike shedding, or rather you students were falling victim to bike shedding. There they discuss trivial matters for a long time and lose track of important matters. While it may be more interesting to hear their story, it won't help you gain important information.

Imagine you were asked to write an essay on Einstein's theory of relativity. The theory of relativity is hard to understand. So you will spend more time writing a few lines about Albert Einstein's personal life and scientific progress.

Bike shedding can negatively affect personal productivity. By resorting to this practice people would be unable to manage their time efficiently. Every day, there are various tasks that we need to complete. Bike shedding results in a disproportionate amount of time being spent on these trivial tasks.

For example, if a day's to-do list includes going to the grocery store, folding clothes, and filing tax forms, people may spend more time shopping for groceries and folding clothes. It is because of the fact that they are simple tasks. Sometimes time runs out when it comes to filing tax forms. As a result of bike shedding, we put off the most important work and waste time doing the easier things on our to-do list.

One way to avoid bike shedding is to hold separate meetings for any important and complex issues. If you come to a meeting with a long agenda, people will be distracted from the main issues. If there is only one purpose and topic of a meeting, it's hard to avoid talking about it. Making meetings specific and focused on a specific topic can help prevent bike shedding. It's a good idea to assign a specific person to hold the team on task and maintain focus if the discussion goes astray.

Another way to focus on specific topics is to limit the number of people in the meeting. By having only the essential people in a meeting, even if the discussion veers off into trivial matters, the overall time wasted will be shorter.

10. Cognitive Dissonance theory

When we hear opposite opinions about something or a person we like, we get very upset. Our minds will work hard to prove this information wrong.

The theory of cognitive dissonance was first introduced by psychologist Leon Festinger. He explains why people are unwilling to change their existing beliefs or behavior in light of new and conflicting information. For example, despite hearing everywhere that smoking causes cancer and many other chronic health conditions, smokers justify their harmful decision to continue smoking. They either reject the evidence supporting its dangers or think that nothing will happen to them alone.

Changing our behavior or beliefs can be difficult, especially if they are deeply ingrained or if these changes can cause discomfort later on. The same goes for smokers. Many smokers are aware of the negative effects of their behavior, but overcoming it leaves them feeling dissatisfied. They are reluctant to accept information that may cause dissatisfaction or difficulty in the future. They cannot change. For a person who is addicted to smoking or drugs, it is very difficult for them to bring about a change of their own. Often it is not possible to do it on its own. This conviction deters them from believing things they do not like.

Rejecting, rationalizing, justifying, or avoiding information that conflicts with our beliefs can lead us to make bad decisions. At this point, we reject information not because it's wrong, but because it makes us uncomfortable. Bare truths and useful information can have the same negative effect on us. Decisions made in the absence of correct and useful information can have harmful consequences. We tend to choose the belief or idea that is most familiar and ingrained in us. We proceed by avoiding situations or information that conflict with existing beliefs.

Cognitive dissonance is one reason why someone believes in a political movement despite the negative performance of the party. When we strongly believe in a political leader or ideology, we are more likely to dismiss information that questions their credibility. In other words, we often ignore or distort evidence that challenges our political beliefs. It is a well- known fact that it is very difficult to change one's mind on political issues. Voters are likely to remain loyal to the same candidate and party, no matter how cleanly presented the evidence that questions the candidate's loyalty.

11. Dunning-Kruger effect

This phenomenon is something that you might have experienced in real life. Assume that you are sitting around the dinner table at a holiday family gathering. Throughout the meal, one member of your extended family boldly declares that everything he says is true and everyone else's opinion is stupid, uninformed, and just plain wrong. He starts talking at length about various topics. The rest of us realize that this person has no idea what he is talking about. But he doesn't let anyone else talk. This effect is named after two social psychology researchers David Dunning and Justin Kruger.

The Dunning-Kruger effect occurs when a person's lack of knowledge and skills in a particular area causes them to overestimate their ability. That means relatively less capable people are ignorant of their incompetence. They may also have the misconception that they are very smart, just as perfectly smart people are not fully convinced of their abilities. On the other hand, those who excel in a certain field find things that are easy for everyone else to be difficult. It also leads to an underestimation of their own abilities.

Let's take a look at some of the great sayings about it:

1. Fools rush in where angels fear to tread - Alexander Pope

2. Ignorance more frequently begets confidence than does knowledge-Charles Darwin

3. The problem with the world is that intelligent people are full of doubt, while stupid ones are full of confidence. (Bertrand Russell)

4. The more I learn, the more I realize how much I don't know. (Albert Einstein)

It is only when we gain knowledge about a subject that we realize how deep that subject is. When we meet people who are very knowledgeable about our subject, we become aware of our shortcomings and we would be eager to learn again. But few wise men speak with great confidence.

As a result of the Dunning- Kruger Effect, you may not realize what you are good at. You are probable to think that what is easy for you is easy for everyone else. So you lose the ability to discover your unique talents and abilities. This effect may lead to poor career choices. So one way to know your abilities is to ask your classmates or teachers "what am I good at?" This is a good tool. This helps you discern when to seek advice from others who view you more objectively than you do while still trusting your abilities.

You will be disappointed when others do not recognize the 'talents' you have discovered in yourself. For example, suppose you are anticipating an upcoming promotion. But to your utter disappointment, someone else gets it. You see your average performance as great while someone who is well- skilled in that area thinks he is just average.

Thinking you're the best at something can cause you to miss opportunities to learn from others who are more skilled or more knowledgeable. Also, thinking that you are average when you have great skills will cost you opportunities to teach and pass on knowledge to others.

Just because you're someone with a research degree in chemistry doesn't mean you're good at biology or economics. And in both these areas, you will be as ignorant as any illiterate. This is one of the main reasons why even those who we think are well-educated continue to forward such nonsense through social media. The majority of people who often take up space on social media, speak in front of a microphone, and make videos on YouTube are not experts in the field. The mistakes of these people are spreading all over the world.

12. Confirmation Bias

Where do your beliefs and opinions come from? Most people assume that their beliefs are rational and neutral. Everyone thinks that they are more logical than others and that their opinions and judgments are the result of years of experience and logical analysis. We often hear people saying that "I have seen a lot of the world and have the maturity of his age.

The truth is that we are all susceptible to a subtle problem known as confirmation bias. We look for and accept only those things that are in harmony with our beliefs. Meanwhile, we completely ignore information that challenges our beliefs.

Confirmation bias occurs when people ignore new information that contradicts existing beliefs. Voters tend to ignore information from news providers that contradicts their existing knowledge. This makes them watch channels with only the same ideas. It is only what we have understood, learned, and wanted to hear over the years that align with our beliefs. We would consciously or unconsciously avoid even scientific truths that challenge our belief systems.

For example, suppose a person believes that left-handers are more creative than right-handed people. Whenever this person meets a left-handed and creative person, the evidence supporting this belief becomes more important. Note that this conclusion is not really based on any statistics. They will not see any examples of many right-handed geniuses and below- average left- hander's.

This bias often creeps into the world of research when psychologists selectively interpret data or ignore negative data in order to produce results that support their initial hypothesis. Remember, people will only ever want to hear and believe again what they know to be in line with their belief system. Most people feel inwardly upset when their knowledge, however flawed, is corrected. For example, suppose you read a very scientific analysis of an event. Your memory sifts through this information like a sieve, retaining only the things you like. Later when you recall the event later, the story becomes completely biased, aligning with your belief system.

Confirmation bias is incredibly prevalent on the Internet, especially on social media. People read online news articles that support their beliefs and fail to seek out sources that challenge them. Various social media platforms, such as Facebook, serve to reinforce people's confirmation bias by providing them with stories they are likely to agree with. This pushes society to extreme political polarization. We are getting trapped in bubbles.

The Psychology of Mind Deception

Some of the effects of confirmation bias can be very harmful, especially in the context of the law. For example, a police officer may have a suspect in mind at the outset of an investigation and later corroborate evidence and fabricate evidence.

13. Decision Fatigue

Why do we make so many bad decisions at the end of the day? Suppose you are forced to make several decisions in one day. With each decision you make, your ability to make a later decision diminishes. Although we generally like to make choices, having to make too many decisions in a short amount of time can lead to bad decisions.

Everyone gets mentally exhausted. In the average adult human, the brain represents about 2% of the body weight. Remarkably, despite its relatively small size, the brain accounts for about 20% of the oxygen and, hence, calories consumed by the body. The phenomenon of decision fatigue can affect even the most logical and intelligent individuals. Each decision we make throughout the day consumes a lot of our mental energy. Then each decision becomes more difficult for us. Ultimately, the brain looks for shortcuts to avoid decision fatigue. This leads to poor decision-making. Decision fatigue affects the choices made by company executives, academic leaders, and politicians. They regularly make choices and decisions that can impact the world on a global scale. Does this make sense?

A prime example is Barack Obama's presidential attire. He revealed that he only wears the same color suits every day to limit the number of decisions he has to make. Obama told Vanity Fair in 2012: "You know I only wear gray or blue suits. I try to minimize the number of decisions I make every day. I don't want to make decisions about what I eat or wear because I have so many other decisions to make." This is a piece of evidence that Obama understands how decision fatigue and the quality of important choices are linked.

This decision fatigue leads some people to avoid making decisions altogether. Big corporate managers who have to make many decisions every day have special training to avoid this fatigue. The level of glucose in your body can affect your decisions. Therefore, if you go shopping in a supermarket when you are hungry, you are likely to buy more than you need. You'll make wiser decisions when you're fresh at the start of the day. To avoid decision fatigue, schedule work meetings and critical decisions early in the day. Proper rest and frequent small meals can help overcome this fatigue.

14. Decoy Effect

This is a phenomenon mainly used in marketing. This way, when the second option is presented to the customer with a less attractive offer, our preference will change between the two options. This second option will be less attractive in all respects than the first option. Compared to these two options, people will choose the third option proposed by marketers.

Let's see how the world's leading magazines use the decoy effect:

Magazines such as The Economist and The New York Times use the decoy effect to promote membership subscriptions. The Economist offered three different types of subscriptions:

1. Web Subscription - $59

2. Print Subscription - $125

3. Web and Print Subscription - $125

People feel the first (web) offer is fair at $59. The second option (print only) seems a little expensive, but the third option, web, and print for the same price as a print-only subscription, seems like a better deal. To further entice subscribers, The Economist offered three subscriptions at the same price.

The cheating effect can cause us to spend and consume more than we really need. If a decoy option exists, we may not make the decision solely based on which option best suits our purposes.

Following our intuition doesn't always lead us to good decisions. Often, the decoy effect leads us to choose the option that costs us more. The deception effect is subtle, but powerful. Once you start to understand how it works, you'll start seeing it everywhere.

Restaurants use the decoy effect when designing menu cards. This design is based on directing the individual to high-profit resources. The 3rd dish on the menu card   in reality is such a decoy. This forces people to choose both the leading resources. The decoy effect is a good example of a psychological attention grabber. This is a type of intervention that 'leads' individuals to make a particular choice. There is no incentive or prohibition for you to do a particular thing here. But some aspects of human nature are abused here.

Every person thinks about themselves as very rational decision-makers. But many such things disturb our reasoning. No one is violating our free will here in decoy effect. It does not impose any restrictions on us. Usually, these deceptions affect us without our knowledge. The idea that our decisions are influenced by factors outside of our awareness can be hard to believe.

15. Choice Overload Effect

Why is the process of selection so difficult when there are so many options?

Choice overload is the anxiety that occurs when you have too much information or options before you have to make a choice. Choosing one will make the other feel wrong, and you'll end up undecided. It is true that more choices will indeed attract more people. But in reality, few choices increase sales.

In a famous study conducted at Columbia University, a research team set up a booth of jam samples. First, they placed 24 jam bottles on the shelf. Every hour they reduced the number from these 24 jams to just six jams. With 24 jams, 60% of customers rushed to get a sample. Only 3% of these consumers bought jam. Only 40% of people showed up when only six jams were shown. But when the choices were reduced, 30% of people bought jam. In other words, consumers have fun seeing everything while being given a lot of options. But fewer choices made them buy it.

In the past, people did not have much choice in matters of marriage, education, work, clothes, and food. Therefore, there was not so much pressure on those in the past. The world has changed a lot with globalization. Today, we have access to products made in every nook and corner of the world. There is a consensus that having more choices gives humans more freedom, and that this is fundamentally good. But ultimately too many choices make our lives difficult and mentally draining. This problem is not only when you go to the store and buy things. Important decisions in life such as education, career, and marriage treatment can all cause this problem. This is because we now have so many options for everything in front of us.

No matter how important they are, choice overload has been shown to delay decision- making. It is because considering the multitude of options available to us greatly exhausts our intellectual systems. Having more options results in less satisfaction with the decisions we make and less confidence in our choices. It also creates the possibility of regretting the decision later. This can significantly affect our mental health and lead to depression, anxiety disorders etc.

16. False Consensus Effect

Social psychologists call the false consensus effect our overconfidence in how well others agree with us. This type of perception bias leads people to believe that their own values and ideas are common among people and that most people have the same opinion. The false consensus effect was first identified and named by researcher Lee Ross and his colleagues in the late 1970s.

The false consensus effect is the idea that other people share the same opinions, beliefs, and behaviors that we do. For example, if you like chocolate ice cream cones, you might think that the world is full of people who like chocolate ice cream cones. Similarly, suppose you are a fan of a particular television show you'd think most people would love that show. This effect can most often occur when certain important opinions, beliefs, and behaviors are considered important.

This trend is very prevalent in social media. For example, suppose Varun's Facebook page consists mostly of posts supporting a particular political party. Varun would think that most of the people in the society have the same type of opinion he had and the majority support that political party. The Facebook algorithm presents feeds in front of you based on your browsing history, past posts, and reactions to other posts. If you are very concerned about the environment, you are likely to overestimate the number of people who are very concerned about environmental issues.

Why does the false consensus effect occur?

One possible cause of the false consensus effect is the availability heuristic. When trying to estimate how common or likely something is, we tend to consider only the examples that immediately come to mind. This effect is strongest in cases where we are certain that our beliefs, opinions, or ideas are correct. If you are 100% convinced that passing a certain law will reduce the level of crime in your community, you are likely to believe that the majority of voters in your town will support the passage of this law.

7. The Empathy Gap

The empathy gap is another cognitive bias that affects our decision making. We have little knowledge of how much our emotions influence our behavior. The empathy gap refers to our tendency to underestimate the influence of different moods on our own behavior and to make decisions that satisfy our current emotion, or state. This makes it difficult for people to perceive their own different states of mind than their current state. They struggle to consider how such external and internal conditions affect people's

judgment and decision-making.

This condition is sometimes referred to as the hot-cold empathy gap. It shows two types of physical condition. 'Hot' emotional states occur when hunger, sex drive, fear, fatigue, or other strong emotions influence our mental state. A 'cool' state of mind is a more logical state. Here our decisions are not influenced by strong emotions. We fail to recognize that whether we are in a hot or cold mood. Our mood influences our reasoning and decisions.

For example you see someone lying on the road. Imagine being asked by the press how you would react here. You, hearing the question, will react very rationally. You say you will help him, give him first aid and take him to the hospital. You are predicting a rational response of your own because you are currently in a 'cold' state of mind because you are not facing that situation now.

In fact, if you were in that real situation, fear and anxiety would make you behave very differently. You will be in a 'hot mood' there. Strong emotions can influence your behavior. This situation shows the empathy gap. The truth is that we cannot predict exactly how we will behave in a particular situation. We predict our future reactions only based on our current emotional states.

Instead of considering the fact that emotions greatly influence our current state of mind, we make every decision based on our limited and short-term present situation. For example you receive a somewhat irritating email from your boss. Suddenly you get very angry. You also reply provocatively without thinking that this anger will cool down after a while, or that he meant something else, or that there will be negative consequences later.

When these emotions do not influence us, we may believe that we have a greater control over our behavior. For example, imagine that you have decided to quit drinking, and one morning, a friend invites you to a party where others are drinking. When deciding to leave for the party, you are not in an emotional state. You believe that you will not enter into temptation. But by the time you get to the party, your emotional state will change and you will be very vulnerable and tempted to drink.

18. Endowment Effect

The endowment effect is equally important in psychology and behavioral economics. When we place a greater value on the things we possess than their actual value, it is called the endowment effect. For example, suppose you bought a ticket for a concert program a few months ago for Rs. 500, but you can't attend the concert. So, you decide to sell that ticket on the black market. You will ask Rs. 550 for the ticket because, as you possessed the ticket for a while, you will feel that the value of that ticket has appreciated. You will feel that you will lose out on selling it at the market price.

The endowment effect affects us both as buyers and sellers. On the one hand, this bias is exploited by marketers. When we feel a psychological ownership over a product, we are willing to spend more on it. On the other hand, as the seller, it can lead to unreasonable pricing based on the false sense that we will lose out if we don't raise the price.

When we get things, we enjoy them, and when we lose them, we grieve. As we hate loss, when we have to make a decision, we tend to focus more on what we lose than what we gain. Suppose you are a trader who normally sells a bucket for Rs. 200. Suddenly, there is a drop in the demand for plastic products. Selling that bucket for less than Rs. 200 when a buyer comes will cause a lot of mental strain on you. But the person who came to buy it is will to pay only Rs. 150 for it. If he buys it, he will be in a conflict. Finally, no sale takes place.

Another possible driver of the endowment effect is the fact that we tend to like more what we associate with ourselves. This is a perceptual bias where we see ourselves in a positive light, and we often believe ourselves to be exceptional in many ways. Research has shown that this view of ourselves extends even to the things we own. This is known as the ownership effect.

Even if an object is not technically ours, we may feel that it is ours somehow. Research has shown that it only takes a very short time for us to develop a sense of ownership over something, which is why people are so reluctant to return anything we lend, including money and books. This psychological ownership can be created very easily. Research has found that allowing people to touch a product before buying it can make people feel a sense of ownership over the item.

When buying a new car, it is common for salespeople to encourage customers to take it for a test drive. Being able to test drive a car before buying is an experience, but these strategies also promote psychological ownership. The more time you use and interact with a product, the more you feel like you own it, and then it is difficult to let it go.

19. Google Effect

The Google effect refers to the tendency to quickly forget information that is readily available through search engines such as Google. This is also known as digital amnesia. This type of information is not stored in our memory because we know that it is easy to get this information online later. For example, suppose you are reading a book and come across an unfamiliar word. You decide to Google the word's definition. A few days later, you see the word again, but you can't remember what it means.

This condition is the Google effect. As all the information is easily available online, we do not keep it in our memory. Google has become an integral part of our daily lives. It was added as a verb in the Oxford English Dictionary in 2006. It's very easy to "Google." You will see the information right there. It should not be memorized. Because of this unconscious thinking, many things do not stay in our memory.

This bias exists not only for what we search for in search engines but also for most information that is easily accessible on our computers or cell phones. Do you remember your parents' or best friend's phone number? The answer is probably no because of the Google effect. The Google effect affects everything we learn, from solving problems to retaining information. Whatever information the internet gives us, it greatly reduces our interaction with the outside world.

Although some believe the Google effect is a sign of technology, there is no evidence that we are getting better at understanding information. Furthermore, there is clear evidence that we do not properly evaluate the information we encounter online. A lot of information on the internet is inaccurate, and it is very dangerous.
The Psychology of Mind Deception

There is not much point in struggling to remember something that can easily be looked up online. But if the quality of that information is poor, that information itself could be dangerous.

As educational institutions increasingly rely on digital methods to conduct research, this Google effect is becoming more pronounced. As the information cannot be memorized, students have to constantly search the internet. This will create a highly dependent state on the digital world. There is a large body of research that suggests that increasing dependence on the digital world can have negative consequences, including inattention, anxiety, reduced performance on cognitive tasks, and reduced social skills.

20. Halo Effect

The word 'halo' is derived from a religious concept. It refers to the circle of light placed around the head of a saint or a holy person to honor their sanctity. The halo effect is a cognitive bias in which positive impressions of people, certain brands, and products in one area lead to an impression of their abilities in another area. Our overall impression of a person gives us an idea of everything about them.

Basically, your overall impression of a person (that they are good) leads you to make a positive assessment of them in all areas. We are quick to judge that a good-looking person is also a good-natured person. Although many factors can influence the halo effect, a person's attractiveness is one of the most common characteristics that create this cognitive bias. Physical attributes such as height, hair, and eye color contribute to perceptions of attractiveness. We judge a person's physical attractiveness as a sign of their success in life and personality.

A consumer's love for a particular product may lead them to choose the same brand-name item when they have to choose between two options. It has a clear impact not only on our personal lives but also on our other decisions. Studies have shown that when the same food products are labeled 'organic' and 'conventional', the 'organic' products receive a higher rating, and consumers are willing to pay more for them.

An example of the halo effect can be found in the field of medicine. Doctors often assume that a patient is healthy from their outward appearance. Remember that without the relevant tests, the doctor can never know for sure whether the patient is completely healthy or not. Another example of the halo effect can be seen in the field of education. Research has shown that students with the most attractive physical attributes or the most attractive names get the highest grades. Even if teachers are experienced, they may still fall into this cognitive trap.

21.Hanlon's Razor theory

This is our inherent tendency to mistake what happens out of the stupidity of a person as his malice. Simply put, some bad things happen often not because people have bad intentions, but because they are least aware of their deeds. For example, if you are not notified about an important event in your company, Hanlon's razor thinking will work for you. You should not assume that this happened because the manager knowingly chose not to inform you. It can be reasonably assumed that they forgot to send it.

Many people are familiar with the difficulty of having a roommate who is difficult to get along with when staying in a hostel. It is very difficult to get along with someone who never washes the dishes, cleans the trash, or stays quiet early in the morning. You may begin to believe that your roommate is intentionally malignant, has a bad personality, or is trying to abuse you.

In such situations, it is important to take a few things into consideration and step back before starting a fight. Is there a reason your roommate does not like you? Do they have a track record of hurting others? If not, try to check if they have a clear understanding of how irritating their actions are to others.

Have you communicated effectively with them to convince them of your difficulties? Are you convinced they know how reckless their actions are? If you have not let them know about the difficulties they are causing you, we all are quick in judging an irritating person as an evil guy. This is Hanlon's razor theory. As a result of this bias, you will try to cut off the relationship as soon as possible.

It is easy to assume that the hurtful actions of others are meant to hurt us, especially when we are susceptible to cognitive biases like the spotlight effect and heuristic influence. The truth is that, in most cases, the other people in our lives lack the awareness or knowledge to understand the impact of their actions. Accepting this truth can help us communicate better and improve relationships with our friends, colleagues, partners, and even our annoying roommate.

Exceptions:
Although Hanlon's razor is very useful advice, it should be applied with caution and common sense. Remember that this razor is not a universal rule, but a heuristic (intellectual shortcut) to help us make decisions. There may be times when it goes wrong. Maybe you have roommates who try to annoy you on purpose. Although it is harmful to assume that all people's unintentional actions are malicious, it is important to clearly understand their actions. When in doubt as to whether an action is malicious or simply

driven by ignorance, it may be helpful to ask yourself the following questions:

- Have I told this person not to do this before?
- Does their behavior change when corrected?
- Will they treat me with respect after that?

It is also not a good idea to blindly assume that others do not understand the consequences when their actions negatively affect you.

22. The Availability Cascade

How information is widely disseminated? For example, a public debate on a topic like climate change suddenly appears on TV. A prominent TV reporter prepares a program on the dangers of this topic when he has no other topic to cover. This leads to further reporting and discussion on the subject, eventually leading the government to legislate to deal with the issue.

In today's environment, it is common for many things to explode and go viral. IT cells can make news and statistics go viral on a massive scale with precise targets. This can change people's mindsets, as people tend to believe what the majority believes, known as the bandwagon effect. People may assume that others think the same way they do and ignore any contrary information.

In 2007, Professors Cass Sunstein and Timur Kuran described how this phenomenon can lead to poor decision-making. In the late 1970s in Niagara Falls, New York, the canal of an old chemical waste dump began to leak. Government officials constantly monitored and tested the level of chemicals in the area. Although it was found that the risk or harmful effects of those chemicals on health were low, a woman named Lois Gibbs began telling her neighbors that the spill was poisoning their entire neighborhood. As the panic spread, politicians joined the popular sentiments, and the canal was eventually declared a disaster. Those who questioned these unscientific claims were accused of not respecting children's health. The government evacuated everyone from the canal area, and hysterical reports in the local and national media spread panic. Decades later, polls show that a majority of Americans consider toxic waste dumps to be the number one environmental problem.

Societies are vulnerable to this flood of bad information. The availability cascade phenomenon is evolutionarily helpful, as one person cannot know everything, and people increase their chances of survival by copying the behavior of others. It is generally accepted that a group of people knows more information than any individual.

23. Functional Fixedness

Functional fixedness is when a person uses an object only in the way it was traditionally intended to be used, and shows an inability to use it in any other way. Functional fixedness kills a person's creativity. This is mainly seen during problem solving. It is common for children to use their imaginations to change many objects for their intended use. Children quickly transform a chair or a cardboard box into pillows, blankets, cars, buses, and forts. As we get older, it becomes very difficult for us to do this.

Imagine someone needs a paperweight but cannot find it. Often, we insist on having a paperweight instead of using a heavy object that could be easily found around the room. Here we will not use a hammer or a glass for this, because our mind will say that those things are not made for that use.

Functional stability prevents companies and societies from innovating and solving pressing challenges. The need to maintain the status quo causes a person to become passive and familiar and do things the same way they have always done in the past. There is comfort in familiarity. It is a natural human tendency to do what is comfortable.

Suppose Elizabeth throws away her plastic food containers immediately after eating. Later, she goes to the supermarket to buy containers for storing things in the kitchen. Elizabeth sees these vessels only as objects for storing food for a certain period of time. If she had not been limited by functional stability, she would have washed and stored these vessels to use them for other purposes.

Functional stability is not really a constant. Self-aware individuals can consciously work to challenge and overcome this bias. By consciously making an effort to think innovatively, anyone can improve their problem-solving skills.

24. Belief Bias

Belief bias is one of the most common forms of cognitive bias. It is very simple. We are more likely to readily accept arguments that are consistent with our belief system. Instead of checking whether a conclusion is logically valid, you accept that conclusion as true because it is plausible to you.

Rather than properly considering the content and structure of that argument belief bias forces people to over rely on their prior beliefs and knowledge when evaluating the conclusions of an argument. People often accept arguments that are consistent with their prior beliefs. They will prioritize their beliefs even if those arguments are weak, invalid, or incorrect. People are often reluctant to accept arguments that contradict their prior beliefs, even when the counterarguments are strong and logical.

An example of a belief bias is that the argument 'All fish can swim, whales can swim, therefore whales are fish' is logical because its conclusion is consistent with their prior beliefs. But this type of argument is not always correct. Just because a whale can swim does not mean it is a type of fish.

25. The fundamental Attribution Error

The Psychology of Mind Deception

Attributing one's actions or behavior to external factors beyond one's control and attributing the actions of other people to their own character or personality. In other words, you find yourself justifying your actions while holding others 100 percent responsible for their actions.

For example, you see a person who is very angry. We are quick to judge that he is hot-headed and arrogant. Perhaps this generally mild-mannered person had experienced some severe trauma that caused him to become angry at the time. You never consider that possibility. But if you are the angry one, you will blame the circumstances entirely.

Think of a 'lazy employee' in your office. One day he comes late for an important meeting. You would be in a hurry to judge his character based on this one incident alone. Remember that his behavior may be due to more external than internal factors. For example, he may be late for a meeting due to a family emergency or some circumstantial reason like a traffic jam.

A decision you make based on something small like this can have far-reaching consequences. If you are the manager and he is your subordinate, you will be judging his performance day after day based on this preconceived notion.

You might have often thought that a colleague should be fired or that a customer care executive is incompetent. But how often have you tried to consider and understand the external factors that might affect this person's work? Often we don't bother about it.

It is difficult to completely overcome this perceptual bias. When you feel resentful toward someone, try making a list of five positive qualities that person exhibits. This will help balance your perspective and help you see your coworker rationally instead of through the lens of a negative lens.

26. Priming Effect

The priming effect is when a person engages with a particular object, and subsequent sensory experiences make him associate another related word to be connected together with the first experiences. It is the positive or negative effect of a rapidly presented stimulus on the processing of a second stimulus. These stimuli are often associated with words or images that people see in their daily lives. As a result of priming exposure to something subsequently changes our behavior or thoughts. For example, if a child sees a bag of candy near a red bench, the child may search for or think about the candy the next time he sees a red bench. Many schools of thought in psychology use the concept of priming

Suppose you hear the word 'doctor'. After a moment, you will recognize the word 'nurse' much faster than the word 'cat'. This is because both medical professionals are connected in your mind.

All this happens without your awareness. The priming effect is usually seen when you are trying to remember the lyrics of a song. If the lyrics of a song are obscure and you struggle to remember them, your brain will fill in the missing information as best it can. Because of the priming effect here, you may not remember the actual lyrics of the song. Many different lines will come to your mind.

When we say apple, depending on the person's association with that particular word, we may think of red color, apple fruit, or Apple's iPhone. The priming effect can have a huge impact on ourselves and those around us in a harmful way. Studies have shown that based on what we read, see, and hear, certain behaviors can be greatly influenced.

John Bargh, a professor, conducted an experiment on students. He asks the students to write some sentences using words that reflect aggressiveness, patience, and positivity. Then, they are told to unscramble those sentences and rewrite them by adding these words. He then asked them to wait for him to check their answers. Burg found that students who were given texts about assault became impatient waiting to check their answers. Students who were given sentences about patience and positivity were more patient while waiting for their answers to be checked. Studies show that if we prime people to act in a certain way, they are more likely to act that way.

Whenever we see a picture of our role model or the power of any of our motivations, it motivates us to work harder and perform better. It influences our behavior. The most relevant example of this is women's empowerment. When women are seen ruling a country or organization, it positively influences women's behavior. Human facial expressions are important social cues in our daily lives. Whenever we see a smiley face, emoji, or any other image, it automatically influences our behavior.

27. Framing Effect Framing Effect

The framing effect is when the same information changes our decisions just because of the way it is presented. Information that is presented more attractively by emphasizing, underlining, and highlighting a text itself is accepted by our mind. Individuals are more sensitive to losses than gains. When presented with a 50-50 chance of winning or losing an equal amount, we avoid such a choice. Because the fear of loss is greater than the joy of gain. People make decisions based on how options are 'framed', that is, whether something is presented as a loss or a gain. People are more interested in things that are presented as benefits. When talking about positive/negative frames let's look at the classic example of a glass half full or half empty. Many marketers use such negative frames to persuade us to buy their products.

"Last chance to make a profit, if you buy it now, you can save a thousand rupees" are examples of this strategy. Losses always hurt us, even if the calculation of a loss and the calculation of a gain is logically and mathematically the same.

If the doctor tells you that a surgical procedure has a 90% chance of success, you agree to that surgery. But if the same doctor tells you that the same surgery has a 10% chance of death, you will be reluctant to agree to it. Logically the two are the same. But the feelings it creates in us are not the same. Of course, we only want to hear the probability of success. When you go to the store and look for a disinfectant, you choose a product that claims to kill 95% of germs. But you would be hesitant to buy a product that says 5% of germs will survive. Remember that both are the same.

Suppose you are concerned about your blood sugar levels. When a drink says it has '10% sugar' you hesitate to buy it. But if it says '90% sugars- free' you choose it. Decisions based on the framing effect depend on how information is presented to us. Bad information or limited options can make us feel better if presented in a positive light.

28. Illusory Correlation

A correlation illusion occurs when two variables (events, actions, ideas, etc.) appear to be related when they are not actually related. For example, John is an avid football fan. He watches all the games played by his favorite 'team' live on television. John always wears their mascot jersey when he watches their games - the same jersey he has worn for years. According to John, wearing 'this lucky jersey' is essential. His team's success depends on it. A few years ago, John noticed that his team lost when he was wearing a different dress. John's false belief that wearing a jersey at home is related to his favorite football team's performance may be due to delusional correlational thinking.

We cannot always know whether two things are causally related and why they happen. We do not seek their cause. It is enough for us to know that it is somehow related. Based on our beliefs we often estimate risks in correlations between different events or behaviors. We may decide that the risk of a road traffic accident is greater during rush hour and that we should not drive.

Suppose you are visiting New York City and someone bumps into your body as you board the subway train. Then, you go to a restaurant. The waiter gets rude to you. Finally, you ask someone on the street for directions and they walk away without saying a word. When you think about your trip to New York, you may recall all these experiences and quickly jump to the conclusion that 'people from New York are rude' or 'people in big cities are rude'.

You don't remember many people in that city being completely normal. You also won't remember the good food you ate. You won't remember hundreds of people walking politely at the train station. It literally becomes a non-event in your mind because it is so unremarkable. As a result, you're more likely to remember the times someone was rude to you than the times you happily ate or rode the metro train peacefully.

Improper correlations may influence countries or institutions to make biased decisions. For example, rare interactions lead to stereotypes and racism. The public tends to exaggerate the violence perpetrated by minorities and makes people think of this violence as being associated with certain races. Although there is no significant correlation between any of these, this thinking prompts countries to resort to stricter immigration controls and stricter deportation practices.

Another perceptual bias, confirmation bias, occurs when we pay more attention to, focus on, and give more credence to evidence that is consistent with our existing beliefs.

29. Identifiable Victim Effect

When disasters strike, if there is a person we can identify with among the victims, we are more likely to feel empathy and be motivated to help them. This is called the identifiable victim effect. When there is a disaster, illness or suffering, if the victim is someone we can identify with, we are more eager and interested in helping them. If someone near our home has an accident or is in need, it affects us emotionally and we go out of our way to help them. But knowing that tens of thousands are dying in other countries or that they are not getting justice would not affect us so emotionally.

Imagine picking up the morning newspaper and seeing two news items:

News 1: All children deserve basic needs and a happy and healthy life. However, many young children across Somalia do not receive this. More than 26 million children suffer from hunger there. This causes them severe pain and emotional and physical stagnation. We need your help to overcome this tragic situation. Make a donation today.

News 2: All children have basic needs and deserve a happy and healthy life. But this is not the case with Varun Prasad in Sarjapur in Bangalore city. Varun is only 12 years old. He is suffering from hunger. He cannot go to school now. He is smaller than other classmates due to stunted growth. Varun needs your help to overcome his dire situation. Make a donation today.

According to the identifiable victim effect, we will be more motivated to help a single starving person, Varun, than the 26 million children we read about in the first story. Although the first story has more suffering, Varun's story evokes our emotions. This increases the likelihood of helping. Because here it is in our country and local city. Moreover, a clear name has been given to identify the victim.

Because of the identifiable victim effect, we tend to compare and exaggerate the hardships experienced by one person to the hardships faced by hundreds or thousands of others. It forces us to distribute money, support, and resources in an ineffective way. This effect leads to a disproportionate amount of resources going to one person instead of distributing it equally to help multiple people overcome the difficulties they face.

The identifiable victim effect demonstrates that our morals are not objective and are often influenced by empathy rather than reason. We are bombarded with statistics about how many people live in poverty, suffer from mental illness, or are victims of violence. But the truth is that none of these statistics evokes enough empathy to make us want to help them.

It is not logical that we should be more willing to help an identifiable victim than we are willing to help a large group of people. Logically and objectively speaking, the tragedy of a large group is much worse than the tragedy of an individual. That is a big threat to humanity itself. More time and resources need to be devoted to reducing that threat. But with the identifiable victim effect, the opposite occurs. That means our present system of philanthropic efforts is often not the most efficient way to help people.

30. Illusion of Control

The illusion of control is the belief that we have greater control over the events around us than we actually have. Even if it is something that happens completely randomly or by chance, we often feel that we can influence it in some way.

As humans we have always tried to control our environment. Early humans built shelters to protect themselves from wind, rain, and snow. Clothes to protect from the cold and headgear to protect from the heat were all designed by man. Primitive humans appealed to the forces of nature in the form of various rituals. They danced, made offerings and performed sacrifices to appease the mysterious forces that controlled the weather. Once it rained by chance or when it started to get cold following a ceremony they believed that their actions influenced the gods. Thus they had the illusion that they have control over the weather.

Illusion of control is a bias in the positive direction. Like the optimism bias, it helps us think more positively about life, even if it is not true. This has been proven in many studies over the years.

Characteristics of the illusion of control

The illusion of control can affect people in a wide variety of contexts and situations. Anytime you think your actions influence an event outside of your personal control, you fall prey to this illusion.

Let's look at some features of this myth:

Engage in rituals: For example, wearing a special lucky item, or participating in rituals such as praying to ensure that your favorite team wins a game.

Dangerous behaviors: People who feel that they are in full control of the events surrounding them are more likely to engage in risky behaviors. People who think that their actions control all events often act very irrationally.

Magical Thinking: Try to make things happen by willpower. That is, imagine changing the traffic light and try to control the basketball player's movements with your own thoughts.

Examples of illusion of control

Once you pick a delicious apple from a basket of apples in the shop. After that you start to think of yourself as a very skilled apple picker. In fact, the whole basket of apples was very tasty. You go into a lottery shop and buy a lottery ticket by looking at some numbers. You hit the prize. You might think you have a special talent for picking lucky numbers. In reality, lotteries are completely random. So you can never influence them with the numbers you choose.

In countries like the United States and Canada, a button is placed on the post to turn on the signal light for pedestrians to cross the road. Those who have to cross the road will be overwhelmed by this. Actually this button has nothing to do with that light. Since the late 80's all traffic signals have been computer controlled. But the city did not pay to remove the buttons. So people feel that they have done something. They help increase people's illusion of control. We feel good when we can do something that seems to have an effect.

Is the illusion of control beneficial?

The illusion of control is often said to be beneficial. Because it will encourage people to take responsibility. When a person is diagnosed with a disease, they want to take control of their disease themselves by starting medication, changing their diet, or other aspects of their lifestyle. Similarly, studies have found that hospitalized patients who are able to self-administer painkillers take lower doses than prescribed by their doctors. They will have less pain.

Feeling that we have control over something can motivate us to do many things even when the odds of success are slim. But this intellectual bias can prevent learning from mistakes and lead to the rejection of opposing views.

The Psychology of Mind Deception

We all wish we could go back and do things differently, change the outcome of an unfortunate event. Many of us are constantly cursing ourselves for what we should and shouldn't be doing. Especially if the outcome of an action is painful, we are tempted to think that it would be different if we could do it again with the knowledge we have now.

Regret for wrongdoing is natural. Not repeating past mistakes is good for growth and maturity. However, dwelling on a past event that cannot be changed is an effect of the illusion of control.

Whatever the circumstances that led to a particular event, those things cannot be changed. In fact, there is no guarantee that we could have changed the outcome even if we had acted differently. The real choice is to move forward with what we have learned from it.

31. Illusory Truth Effect

When we hear false information over and over we would be force to believe it to be true. This is because of the illusion of truth. According to a 2015 study in the Journal of Experimental Psychology, the illusion of truth is the perception that repeated statements are truer than newly presented statements. This effect is well understood by marketing professionals, religious leaders, and politicians. In other words, even if something is a lie, if you assert it repeatedly, people will start believing it.

Joseph Goebbels was Nazi Germany's Minister of Propaganda. Let us look at some of his basic rules. "Never allow the public to become emotionally cold, never admit any wrongdoing on our part, never assume that there is any good in the enemy, never give any room for alternative thoughts, never blame yourself, focus on one enemy at a time and blame him for everything that happens around him. People will definitely believe you".

Ultimately even if we are previously convinced that a piece of information is false, this illusion can come to haunt us.

How do we know if a campaign is right or wrong? Naturally, we will compare that information with the evidence available to us. Sometimes we may resort to Google searches. Each person thinks that he is the one who judge's things based on logical facts. Unfortunately, humans rarely think rationally. Every day, we make many decisions. A lot of information is coming at us in a short period of time. Our brains cannot process this information as deeply as we would like. To conserve our limited mental energy, we rely on countless shortcuts known as heuristics to make sense of the world. This often leads us to make mistakes in our decisions.

An advertising that repeats unsubstantiated claims about a product may increase sales. Because some viewers may think they heard these claims from an objective source. This effect is also used in news media. This is an important part of political campaigning.
The Psychology of Mind Deception

Take the examples of advertisements about health drinks. They show a model wearing a doctors coat saying -listen to the doctor; he recommends our product. But we tend to believe this.

According to renowned behavioral psychologist Daniel Kahneman, our brain has two thinking systems.

System 1 is fast and automatic. They work without our awareness. System 2 handles deeper and more demanding operations. It is within our conscious control. It is laborious, difficult and energy-sapping. We do not like that. So, wherever possible, we try to rely on System 1.

In this age of social media, misinformation spreads rapidly to large numbers of people at an incredible speed. All they have to do to get a lie to be believed is to repeat it over and over again. Evidence suggests that online disinformation campaigns are already strongly influencing global politics. It threatens the integrity of democracy and the cohesion of our societies. People who are interested in fact checking and verifying hate campaigns might have noticed something. The same sentences or paragraphs related to propaganda would be posted in thousands of social media handles.

32. Extrinsic Incentive Bias

This perceptual bias causes us to view every action of others with an eye of suspicion. We tend to assume that someone doing or learning something new is only for extrinsic benefits such as job security or higher wages. We never admit that their purpose is to develop new skills or to gain self-esteem or self-satisfaction from an intrinsic motivation.

"I work overtime because I am dedicated to my work. But my colleagues work overtime to make more money." - An example of this is a worker who thinks like this.

People are often negative. Most of the time we do not take into account the great motivation that the other person has. We will never accept such a fact. We tend to think that money or greed drives people to the stock market, that all politicians are power-hungry, and that people post on social media only for getting likes. But if these same people were asked about the motivations for their own actions, their answers would be just the opposite. Bankers say they are fascinated by markets, and politicians say they are happy to make a difference in society. They say they post photos on Social media to maintain social connections with others.

A survey was conducted in the mid-nineties. Around 500 law students participated in this survey. When asked about their motives for studying law, 64% said the reason was the intellectual appeal of law. On the other hand, only 12% believe that their peers share the same motivation. 62% stated that their classmates are driven by money.

There is no clear cognitive explanation for why we exhibit an extrinsic motivation bias. However, one theory of this is that we are always trying to positively elevate our own behavior in comparison to others. Behavior based on money does not reflect well in modern society. It is comfortable to think and say that they are different and that other people are not.

33. Illusion of Validity

Illusion of validity is a cognitive bias that describes our tendency to be overconfident that we can arrive at accurate predictions by interpreting a given set of information or statistical data.

Have you ever played online number games? A number may have come repeatedly in the betting cycle. You notice that. Each number has an equal chance of coming up, but you assume that this number is less likely to come up again on the next roll or spin. Many people fall victim to this bias and end up losing money at casinos. This is a phenomenon called the illusion of validity.

Teachers often believe that they can accurately predict how well a student will do in their course based on their past performance in school. Suppose a teacher is very confident in their predictions about a certain student. But many things may happen in his real life that leads him in a different direction. For example, if the student begins to experience symptoms of a mental illness such as depression, or if they witness a parent's divorce, they are more likely to do poorly academically. On the other hand, a student who usually gets low grades may work hard, knowing that the college program he wants to enter is quite competitive. In both cases the teacher may have predicted the performance of the student in their class based on a pattern before them. All these predictions could go wrong.

The unpredictability of the world we live in makes us uneasy. So we keep trying to find a coherent explanation for random events. We fill in the gaps as needed by inferring cause and effect from the information readily available to us. It is easy to weave a satisfying story with the little information we have. It can lead us to believe that we know more than we realize.

Psychological-forensic experts such as Cassim, Meissner, Norvik, Lassiter, Clerk Daniels and others conducted a psychological experiment in 2005 on college students and experienced police officers. In a survey of a panel of American forensic experts and Canadian customs officials, 77 percent of people said they could accurately identify criminals on seeing them. These experiments showed that police officers were no more skilled or proficient than average college students in detecting whether someone was lying when they made a false confession.

In another experiment, a recorded confession of a non-suspect was played to police and college students. A good percentage of the police believed him to be a criminal. But a large percentage of the students doubted his innocence. From this it should be understood that there is a biased thinking among policemen to think that people are criminals.

Our predictions often influence the decisions we make. Especially when we feel confident in a prediction, we are more inclined to make important decisions based on it. When these predictions go wrong, there are unfortunate consequences.

See a study by Oskamp (1965). Participants in this study were clinical psychologists and graduate students. The experimenters asked these groups to predict the reasons for each patient's visit to that hospital. They were asked to make out the reason to be Psychological problems or some other medical cause. The researchers found that there was no significant difference in the accuracy of the predictions made by these two groups. Experienced clinical psychologists were only marginally better at making predictions than untrained undergraduates. The experimenter Oskamp explained that the clinical psychologists later recalled only those instances in which their predictions were correct. At the same time they ignored the wrong predictions made earlier. We remember only the correct predictions we made and forget the wrong predictions.

Overconfidence is an undesirable trait for its consequences are often far-reaching. It is often unfortunate when it applies to people in positions of power, such as politicians or police officers, who have to make important decisions that affect the lives of many others.

34. Inattentional Blindness

It is logical to think that we see everything around us while our eyes are open. We would never believe when someone says that the image of the object had fallen on the retina, still you did not see that. But the reality is that attention plays an important role in the experience of seeing. This is one of the main reasons you fail to notice obvious mistakes in movies. This is a psychological phenomenon known as Inattentional Blindness.

You may often not notice things that come unexpectedly into your field of vision. We have great confidence in our observation skills and what we see and understand. Most people think that we capture what is in front of our eyes like a camera. But in reality we see very little of what unfolds before our eyes. Very little of what we see is processed by our brain. Only a little of what goes inside reaches our conscious mind. Even less remains in our memory.

A teenager, for example, drives a car along a familiar highway. He is very attentive to the speedometer, rear view mirror and oncoming traffic. Suddenly he sees a deer standing on the road. He hits the brakes, but goes late. He hits the beast. His parents suspected inattention was the cause of the accident. The teenager insists that his full attention was on the road. In fact, his focus was only on driving and even then he never saw the deer.

When you are driving while talking on your phone, other vehicles and people right in front of you would not come to your notice. The human brain can only handle one thing at a time. Our brain is a microprocessor which cannot multitask. It can do only batch processing. That is only one process could be handled at any single point of time. When we talk on the phone and drive, the brain's attention alternates between the phone and the car. Let us say that at the microsecond of your attention shifting from driving to the phone call, you would not even notice even if a child jumps in front of your car.

Your view is actually just a keyhole view especially when you are preoccupied. It does not mean that you see everything when you are completely relaxed. Many things must have come before our sight and our gaze might have fallen on them. But many things do not reach the level of our memory. But this is not a very rare occurrence. And it is hard to believe that we haven't seen much of what we've seen.

The invisible gorilla

This is an experiment done by American psychologists Dr. Christopher Chabris and Dr. Daniel Simons. The experimenter asks a group of students dressed in white and black to pass a basketball to each other. They ask the spectators to count the number of times the ball has been passed by the men dressed in black. Meanwhile, a man dressed as a gorilla passes between them. When asked how many of the viewers of this video have seen the gorilla, 50% of people agree that they have never seen such an ape come and go. This video is on YouTube (The Invisible Gorilla). Change blindness is the twin brother of inattentional blindness.

The truth is that we often do not even notice even if something we saw moments ago has changed so much. In many films, there would be three or four changes in costumes and locations in one scene. But most people do not care about it.

In another experiment conducted by Dr. Simon, Dr. Daniel Levin ,they showed a group of people a video of a conversation between two actresses. One actress is shown first and then another actress is shown speaking. In between, the color of her clothes, the food she eats, and so on make nine changes in this video. When asked if they had noticed any changes or what things had changed, the majority responded that they had not noticed any changes. After that they show the same video. This time they were informed that there were some changes taking place in the video. Even when the video was shown again, they could notice only two changes out of nine. 33 percent of people did not even notice that the actress had changed.

The Psychology of Mind Deception

There are many theories that try to explain why we experience this type of cognitive bias. Certain sensory stimuli (such as bright colors) and cognitive stimuli (such as something familiar) are more likely to capture your brain. So we may miss sight that does not fall into either of these two categories.

Another theory is that when our mental energy is focused on one particular thing, most of our cognitive resources are used up and other stimuli cannot be absorbed. That being said, we do not have the ability to absorb multiple stimuli at the same time.

35. Hyperbolic Discounting

Hyperbolic discounting is a psychological bias that misleads us. Here people prioritize immediate reward and gratification over future gain. Companies use this strategy in sales and marketing to encourage consumers to buy goods based on short-term reward or instant gratification. For example, suppose someone says that he can give you 500 rupees now or 2000 rupees in 6 months. Given a choice like this, most people would choose the first option.

Varun buys lottery tickets every week. One day he wins the lottery of 20 lakhs. Varun ran to the lottery office to claim his prize. The lottery director gave him a choice, either claim 5 lakhs now or opts for the option of getting 2 lakhs every year for the rest of his life. Varun is only 35 years old now. Even if he lives only till the age of 55, he will get Rs 40 lakh. That is twice what it is getting now. But

Varun is dreaming of the money that will soon be in his bank account, and he is counting on the things he can buy. Varun decided to take the first option, even though it would pay more in the long run.

There is an e-commerce selling method called 'after pay'. This is a way in which customers can buy goods now and pay later-a scheme where they pay a part of the amount due upfront and pay the balance in monthly installments. Buying a new TV is expensive. The 'after pay' system allows them to delay their immediate financial burden. They can buy the things they need without having to pay the entire amount up front. You will receive the item immediately. This positively impacts people's income over time.

Hyperbolic discounting can have devastating effects in many aspects of life, not just in marketing strategies and advertising. For example, hundreds of thousands of people undergo coronary artery bypass graft procedures each year. This surgery saves their lives. However, it is possible to maintain their quality of life in the long term only by adopting the right lifestyle changes. Unfortunately, people do not take the changes that doctors recommend at face value, such as stopping drug use, eating a healthy diet, and taking medications faithfully. Statistics indicate that ninety percent of sufferers resort to unhealthy diets and lifestyles for short-term pleasure. Credit cards are another pernicious thing. Credit cards maximize hyperbolic discounting.

Hyperbolic discounting can lead people to make poor decisions for it gives excitement and instant gratification. We make decisions that prioritize short-term gratification and distract from our long-term well-being. Hyperbolic discounting can blind us to the benefits of long-term decision-making.

36. In-Group Bias

Are you a sports fan? So how do you feel when you see someone wearing your favorite club's jersey or someone supporting your team? It is indeed a very good feeling, isn't it? When you travel abroad, how happy you feel when someone says they are from your state or your hometown. It is natural to feel more confident and secure when we know like-minded people are around us.

What happens when you meet someone from the opposing sports team? It will make you feel uncomfortable. Why is this happening? This is called in-group bias. It is also known as in-group favoritism or intergroup bias. It is our tendency to be more helpful and positive towards members of our own group than members of other groups. Let us look at some real life examples of such group identities. These include ethnic groups, political ideological groups, religious belief groups and geographical identities. In-group bias can also be seen in artificial laboratory settings. When participants in an experiment are randomly separated into arbitrary groups.

Suppose you are a football fan. Brazil is your favorite team. At work, suppose you have two colleagues who are interested in football. John is a fan of the Brazil team. Julie is a supporter of the Argentina team. Apart from sports interests, Julie and you have many things in common. But you would probably be more interested in John than Julie.

This group bias can harm our relationships with people who do not belong to our same group. Our tendency to favor in-group members may lead us to treat others unfairly. It creates in us a tendency to view the behavior of people who do not belong to our group with intolerance. Cross-cultural studies have found that we may feel justified in doing immoral or dishonest acts to benefit our group.

This means that the tendency to criticize members of one's own group or culture more harshly than members of out-groups is more common among members of minority groups. A study of children found that boys were more fair to their own group from ages 3-8. Whereas girls did not show such tendencies. Oxytocin is the hormone that causes us to feel attracted to people with similar characteristics.

The Psychology of Mind Deception

37. Nostalgia Effect

People remember the past more fondly due to a cognitive bias called the nostalgia effect. We often think that the past was much better than it actually was. Feelings of nostalgia or sentimentality make us place more value on our past social relationships and not look at things purely based on money. Memories of the past can make us spend more on products. Nostalgia weakens our desire to save money, an effect that fosters social ties.

Suppose one day you see a friend's old pictures on Facebook. That old photo itself makes you feel good. We get emotional when we see blurry, sepia-toned photos in our feed. Even if we do not know the people in those pictures, it gives us a good experience. Old hairstyles, shirts, school/colleges and old songs will give you nostalgia of memories.

Let us look at some of the statements made about homesickness by studies conducted in the Journal of Personality and Social Psychology:

1. When someone shares a nostalgic experience, the person telling the story is often the hero of the story.

2. Nostalgic narratives contain more positive emotions than negative ones.

3. Nostalgia is a response to negative moods and feelings of loneliness.

4. People use nostalgia to strengthen social relationships, increase positive self-esteem, and generate positive emotions.

Why does nostalgia make us spend more money?

Studies show that there is a link between nostalgia, social relationships and our desire for money. Nostalgia is the reminiscence of good experiences. It helps individuals look back on memories with complete positivity. So nostalgia fosters social bonding, reduces loneliness and increases social connections. After the release of a campus movie, the students of many colleges would be motivated to hold a reunion. That is, we will pay money for anything that gives pleasure to the mind.

Nostalgia is an important tool used by marketing teams and by using it effectively they can significantly increase the sales of certain products. Companies often use nostalgia to their advantage. They advertise their products in a way that evokes nostalgia.

38. Lag Effect

The Psychology of Mind Deception

When a lot of information is presented to us repeatedly and there are long gaps between the information, the information stays in our mind longer. This phenomenon is called the Lag Effect.

While you are at work, your wife texts you on the way back- a reminder to buy clothes that have been dry-cleaned. To remember this, you repeat to yourself three times, 'Buy the dry-cleaning when you come home from work.' Then you continue with your work. But when you get home, your partner asks you where the dry-cleaned clothes are. You wonder how come you forgot it after repeating it so many times?

According to research, continuous repetition is not actually the best way to remember information. The lag effect suggests that the longer the time between repetitions of information, the more likely that information will remain in our memory. That is, instead of repeating 'buy dry-cleaning after work' three times together, it would have been more likely to be remembered if it had been said every hour.

Many studies have shown that this delay effect is of great importance in learning. For example, right before an exam we review information quickly and repeatedly. We read and recite the same thing over and over again. But we forget many things learned like this later.

It may seem more logical to us that if information is repeated immediately, it is more likely to be committed to memory. But we can achieve more by being aware of the delay effect in the field of learning. Teachers should be able to give sufficient time in between while repeating the material being learned. This gives students more opportunity to retain information. Teachers can hold revision sessions to increase the delay between repetitions or combine information with other activities that children need to remember.

39. Mandela Effect

The Mandela effect is when a person believes that something actually happened based on their distorted memories. They can vividly remember events that happened completely differently or things that never happened. The truth is that there is no lying or cheating in the Mandela Effect. A large crowd will believe that an event never happened in the Mandela Effect.

Origin of the Mandela Effect

The term 'Mandela effect' was first coined by Fiona Broom in 2009. They even created a website detailing this phenomenon. Broome was speaking at a conference. She spoke about how she remembers the news of former South African President Nelson Mandela's death in a South African prison in the 1980s. In fact, Nelson Mandela did not die in prison in the 1980s. He died in 2013 after being released from prison and becoming the president of that country. When Broom started talking to others about his memories, they realized he wasn't alone. Others then recalled seeing the news of his death and his widow's speech.

Some Mandela effects examples

1. O+ve blood group is the universal donor.

It's not taught in classrooms but still most people have this wrong fact engraved in their mind:

O-ve is the universal blood donor

2. National Language of India : Hindi

No. India does not have a national language. India has 22 official languages.

3. National Sport of India: Hockey

No. India does not recognize any particular sport as a 'national game.' We did well in the Olympics from 1928 until 1980. Because of its success, hockey has so long been known as the national sport of India but No.

4. Mickey Mouse might be the most famous cartoon character in the world, but even Disney's famous mouse is often misremembered in the minds of fans. People often report the character wearing suspenders when he does not.

Reasons for Mandela Effect

a. Wrong memory

In psychology, false memory is a phenomenon in which someone remembers something that did not happen or remembers it differently from what actually happened.

b.False reporting

How many times have you heard fake news that your favorite celebrity has died? Whether it is intentional or accidental, reporting false news can lead people to believe something which is not true. Social media, which is quick to spread rumors, exacerbated the problem. Because here anyone has the opportunity to spread anything.

It is common for many people to give different accounts of the same event. We notice that the same person gives different types of information about the same thing at different times. We often interpret this as a story-telling trick that a person intentionally makes. The attributes and credibility we give to our memory are completely unrealistic. Memory is not something that captures things like a digital recorder, preserves them in perfect perfection, and retrieves them without a scratch. Our memory is just a collection of images, information and feelings scattered here and there. This information may be revised from time to time. Our experiences, our mental, physical, and health conditions, our beliefs, our education and a lot of other factors influence the rewriting and editing of these memories.

40. Leveling and Sharpening

Leveling and sharpening is a process that occurs when you retell a story that happened in your life. It is a process of exaggerating some of the emotional parts of the story and filling in some of the blanks with credible information.

You may be surprised to hear a friend retell a funny situation that happened to them years ago. They probably won't tell the whole story in detail. Some unimportant details may be left out. Also, the dialogue in the story and the details of the people involved may be changed. Sometimes a drama can be added to the story. This is done to keep the audience interested.

Narrators choose many memories from the past. Sharpeners tend to select a few memories and discard many as they absorb new knowledge. Leveling is when we drop certain things in our memory, thinking they are 'minor' details. But sharpening means the exaggeration and extreme inclusion of small details that add a lot of meaning to the overall narrative.

Both recall and sharpening are commonly associated with the concept of selective memory especially when it comes to storytelling and narration. Suppose you are telling a friend a funny story about how you tripped and fell in public. You may exaggerate certain aspects to create a sense of drama. For example, you would say that many people saw the fall. But in reality it was a very busy street and most people did not notice it. You might miss many small details like this. Paraphrasing and sharpening bring out our deepest cognitive biases. For example, when telling a story we may use dilation and sharpening to satisfy our confirmation bias. We may remember information that is consistent with our personal belief or opinion and ignore information that contradicts it.

Suppose you have the opinion that dogs are dangerous and unfriendly animals. One day you see a dog barking loudly in the park. You may tell several people a story that confirms your belief that the dog is a dangerous animal. In reality the dog may have been far away from you and under the watchful eye of the owner. Or maybe it was playing with another dog. You do not mention these facts.

Leveling and sharpening play an important role in individual decision making. Although we are not aware of this perceptual bias, it is true that every time we make a decision, new information and stimuli come into us. At the same time we compare this information with the memories and experiences stored in our brain. As a result, psychologists believe that people who engage in

The Psychology of Mind Deception

flattening and sharpening have an advantage in learning and decision-making. Because they can make more accurate decisions.

41. Noble Edge Effect

The noble edge effect is the reputation that a company acquires by donating to charity or supporting socially responsible causes. Due to this effect, customers seek the company's products and services. When customers perceive a company as superior, they show a special interest in buying its products. And they will tell others good things about this company.

We see companies that are founded with an emphasis on social responsibility and mission as symbols of greatness. The profits they make are second-guessed. Consumers always like to see the charitable side of companies. But we won't accept companies bragging about it. If they do, everything they do will be in vain. Just as every author thinks his book is the best ever, every company thinks their philanthropy makes them famous. People want to hear it all from someone else, not from them.

A study by social psychology researchers Blair and Chernev states: A consumer's perception of a company's good deeds influences the way it evaluates that company's product. This is what a human wine tasting experiment revealed. A group of people were recruited into the experiment after learning that the wine company donates a portion of their profits to charity. They did not communicate this to the other group. All participants were non-wine experts. First group of wine connoisseurs rated the wine highly. The idea that the company was giving money to charity motivated them.

We see an ad on TV that mentions the fact that they donate a portion of their profits to charity. But we see it as a cheap marketing ploy. Suppose we later see an ad for a particular charity and they thank a particular company for their donations. We will appreciate it and be interested in buying that company's products.

42. Omission Bias

Omission bias is the tendency of the human mind to overlook a harmful omission and view a harmful act as a grave mistake. Although both are equally harmful, our mind perceives harmful actions as more serious. For example, a person sets fire to a house. This is an example of an act of violence. No doubt. Another person saw this fire. But he does not call the fire force or inform the locals. This is an example of harmful exclusion. Are they not equally responsible for the fire? Even though the consequences are in fact the same (the fire caused more damage), due to avoidance bias the person who lit the fire will be judged more harshly than the person who watched it and did not move.

Generally, most people want to do good in their daily lives and not harm anyone. Every person wants to be benevolent and compassionate. Our internal moral barometer prompts us to act accordingly. However, it goes without saying that sometimes the moral judgments we make are based on biased thinking. Both of them have negative consequences. In similar situations, avoidance bias causes us to view harmful actions as worse than omissions (instances in which someone fails to take action).

Scenario 1: You are walking down the footpath of a busy street. You see a man walking while looking at his phone and texting. He does not look at the road. You see him step in front of a speeding vehicle. But you stand there silently. He gets hit by a car and dies.

Scenario 2: You are walking on the same footpath. He is busy chatting on the phone. Infuriated by his behavior, you push him into the busy street. You watch as he falls to his death.

In which of these situations did you make the more damaging decision? In fact both resulted in the same result, the death of a pedestrian would be judged as a grave crime. But if you believe that pushing someone into traffic is the only harmful decision, then you are ruled by an avoidance bias.

The reluctance of most parents to vaccinate their children is the potential for harm or side effects from the vaccine. However, research shows that the risks to your children if they get the disease outweigh the side effects of vaccinations.

When someone is killed in police brutality, only the policemen who are directly responsible for it come before the law. But the violence could have been stopped by many policemen who were watching these atrocious deeds. Aren't they equally guilty? Avoidance bias places a limit on our moral responsibilities. If the harmful actions had more gravity, we would not be disturbed by the harm caused by our omissions.

Enact a law that requires everything possible to be done to save a life. But the situation is now that if someone fails to save a life in the act of doing so, they are punished for negligence.

43. Optimism Bias

Optimism bias is the tendency to overestimate the likelihood of positive events in our lives and underestimate the likelihood of negative events.

A little bit of optimism is very necessary. It makes us persevere in the face of difficulties and rejections. It helps us to believe in our own abilities. It inspires us to focus on the positive instead of dwelling on the negative. However, this optimism can blind us to counter-effects and lead to poor decision-making. As humans we tend to overestimate the positive events in our lives. We consider ourselves rational beings. But there are times when we are too optimistic for our own good.

Optimism bias is the false belief that we are more likely to have positive events in our lives than others and less likely to experience undesirable events. In other words, we overestimate the likelihood of positive or happy events occurring. This bias can lead to wrong life decisions.

Let's look at some very common optimism biases:

1. Not keeping cash for emergencies as your job is considered very secure

2. Companies not having a risk management plan in place. Because they underestimate the risks

3. Believing that just because you graduated from a reputed institute, you are hundred percent sure to get a good job.

Some factors that can cause optimism bias are:
Rare occurrences: People think that cyclones and floods are less likely to affect them as they are not common everyday occurrences. People feel more optimistic when they think that these events are under the individual's direct control and influence. People believe that things will work magically. It adds excessive faith in God and a sense of dependence.

Optimism bias is more likely to occur when something is seen as unlikely. For example, if a person believes that skin cancer is very rare, he is likely to be unrealistically optimistic about those risks. A question many people ask when dealing with a disease like cancer is why did I get it? People do not think that something that can happen to anyone has happened to them too.

Some factors that dampen optimism include:
Experiencing certain events in reality can reduce optimism. People are less likely to feel optimistic when they compare themselves to close loved ones, such as friends and family members, who are going through hardships. Research published in 2011 showed that people with depression or anxiety have a lower optimism bias.

44. The Just-World Phenomenon

The just-world phenomenon refers to the belief that this world is just and therefore our actions and moral conduct determine our outcomes. This view leads us to believe that those who do good will be rewarded and those who do wrong will be punished. People want to believe that the world is fair, so when they see an injustice taking place they will look for ways to justify, explain, or rationalize it. This theory often leads people to blame the victim.

Just-world theory and victim blaming
When people suffer misfortune, others have a tendency to investigate their role in the failure. In other words, people have an automatic tendency to blame someone when unfortunate events

happen. Instead of saying that a bad turn of events and adverse circumstances caused this misfortune, people blame the actions of the victim for the misfortune.

On the contrary, this belief makes people think that when good things happen to them, they are good and deserve good luck. Because of this, extremely lucky people often seem more deserving of their good fortune. Instead of attributing their success to luck or situational favors, people attribute that luck to the person's inherent characteristics. People often think of these people as more intelligent and hardworking than the unfortunate ones. Research published in 2012 suggests a strong link between just-worldview and religiosity.

People blame the poor for their living conditions and lifestyles. People blame rape victims for their behavior and clothing.

Why does the just-world phenomenon occur?
People never like to think that they will ever be the victim of a violent crime. Therefore, when hearing about an incident such as assault or rape, people may try to blame the victim's behavior. Many people think that by avoiding certain behavior, they can avoid becoming victims of that crime themselves. People never want to face a scary situation.People believe nature as a divine force which is so just.They never could perceive the idea that nature could cause any harm to any living beings. People want to reduce anxiety caused by injustices in the world. Believing that

each individual is solely responsible for their own misfortune, people can believe that the world is fair and just.

45. Illusion of Justice

The illusion of justice is the notion that our natural sense of justice is the true way of the world. Our natural sense of justice compels us to accept that good is rewarded and evil is punished. Our natural sense of justice makes us reject bad things that happen to good people and good things that happen to bad people. It goes against our natural sense of justice when we see that bad behavior is rewarded well or good behavior has the opposite effect.

"If I'm kind to you, I expect you to be kind to me. I don't expect you to cheat on me, and you don't expect me to cheat on you." We hear these phrases all the time. But in the real world, we regularly see good, bad, despicable, and indiscriminate things going on, and crooks routinely get away with their misdeeds.

It is true that to some extent, we can avoid diseases. For example, lifestyle habits such as following good nutritional habits, exercising regularly, avoiding smoking and excessive alcohol consumption are good for maintaining good health. So if a person who has smoked cigarettes for forty years is diagnosed with lung cancer, we should not be surprised. We would assume that natural justice was served. We would never digest the fact that there is just a causal relationship between his smoking habit and cancer. If someone you know has been defrauding his customers for years and is finally caught and sent to jail, you won't feel sorry for him. But those who live very carefully, eat moderately, exercise regularly, do not drink, do not smoke, get cancer, we feel terribly upset. Suppose a man who lives an orderly life, stands in a waiting shed by the roadside, out of the rain. If a speck of asbestos gets into his body and the effect causes him to develop cancer, you will find it very difficult to find justice. Likewise, you may find it hard to accept the fact that 25 years of smoking did not cause cancer.

Humans think that everything has a reason, that there are no coincidences or accidents, and that justice always prevails. We may not know exactly why some people get cancer or lose their jobs. But we firmly believe that it is the result of karma and that this world is just.
We can only believe that truth, dharma, justice and goodness will be the final victory and those who do evil will be the victims of nature's wrath in the end. The idea that we ourselves will suffer the consequences of our actions is good for society to some extent.

46. The Backfire Effect

Why don't we change our misconceptions even when we get the right facts?

In a perfectly rational world, we would assume that people would correctly evaluate evidence that challenges their false beliefs, and then change their false beliefs accordingly. In fact, this is something that rarely happens. We only read, learn and accept what we believe and want to believe. This is called conformation bias.

When people are presented with evidence that causes them to doubt their beliefs, they often reject this evidence and strengthen their support for their original position. This is caused by an intellectual bias known as the backfire effect. Have you noticed a slight change in anyone's opinion or belief in any discussion or argument? Each person tries to oppose the other's arguments and correct the counter-arguments. Therefore, no matter how many scientific proofs and arguments you present, you cannot change a true believer from his beliefs.

Backfire effect affects your ability to change the opinions of others as well as your ability to rationally convince yourself of true information. The backfire effect is a curious reaction. When people are presented with evidence against their beliefs, their old beliefs become stronger again. The backfire effect has been observed in many scientific studies.

Let us look at a study conducted in Britain. Exposing people to negative information about a political candidate they like often increases support for that candidate. When presented with misconceptions about politically important issues, it made people believe more strongly in their true misconceptions.

Being aware of this effect can greatly reduce your own backfire effect. You could respond when you hear information that contradicts your beliefs. When you hear negative information, do not completely ignore it or try to explain why it is wrong. Instead, you should look at it with a new mind. Evaluate the new information based on its logic rather than comparing it to your previous theory on the subject.

There is something called the familiarity backfire effect. If a person is proven wrong about something they believe, at first they may believe it and accept it, but after a while they forget it and believe the same old things. No matter how many times people are convinced that many false theories about health are wrong, they will eventually accept what they once believed.

This does not mean that no one changes their opinion. There is no point in trying to change a person of a firm belief especially if he is also a propagandist of that belief. But people with a slightly open mind can be swayed by scientific arguments. Our brain is not a neutral truth-seeking machine. When a person is in a good mood, he is more open to opposing ideas.

47. Illusion of Explanatory Depth

It is an illusion that we understand more than we actually do about many things. It gives people false confidence. It is only when we are asked to explain something that we will realize how little we know about it.

Let us look at another aspect of Illusion of explanatory depth. We mistake our familiarity with a situation for an understanding of how it works. Many employees who have been working in hospital jobs for years assume they know as much as a doctor. So is the subject of psychology. A lot of people say, 'I know a lot of psychology'. People have the impression that psychological knowledge is too simple or obvious. This illusion is related to the Dunning-Kruger effect.

The more people self-rate their knowledge, the stronger this illusion becomes. Even though this effect (overestimation of knowledge) applies to almost everyone, it mostly affects people who are not very knowledgeable. People rate themselves as highly knowledgeable when they know that knowledge of a particular subject is highly valued in society.

An alien is coming to Earth. Imagine that it asks you to explain the concept of houses. The concept of houses is very easy to explain, right? You live in a house now and see at least 50 houses every day when you walk or drive. So when an alien asks, you can tell him what a house is. But the truth is, you would not be able to explain much about it. What are the rules pertaining to houses? How is a house built? How much will it cost? How many days will it take to build a house? So he will have more questions that you cannot answer. If you have so many doubts about something so trivial, how little would you know about complex things?

The Illusion of explanatory depth encourages people to take extreme political positions when they are clearly ill-informed about an issue. Asking people to explain a topic can dispel this illusion. For example, do not ask a guy why you believe in the Communist Party. Instead they should be asked to explain about communist ideas, Karl Marx ,Das Capital or Communist Manifesto. Many would be confused without answers to such questions.

48. Ostrich Effect

 Ostriches are a bird that is considered ridiculous. Contrary to the popular myth, ostriches do not bury their head in the sand when scared or frightened. In fact, when an ostrich senses danger and cannot run away, it will flop to the ground and remain still, attempting to blend in with the terrain. Burying their head in the sand when scared is completely stupid as a defensive strategy.

The ostrich effect is a cognitive bias that causes people to avoid negative information, including feedback that helps them monitor their progress. Instead of understanding the facts and dealing with adversity, people bury their heads in the sand like ostriches. There is a saying that 'he closes his eyes and pretends to be dark around'. This avoidance of reality often makes matters worse. If things are not dealt with in time, we will have to pay a heavy price.

Let us see how Ostrich affects personal health. Fear of receiving bad news about their health keeps people from getting blood tests and seeing doctors. They cause many dangers that could have been avoided if they had been examined and treated on time. Some people avoid negative information to protect their self-esteem. They pretend they did not see the unpleasant information in order not to destroy the self-image they have created.

Not looking at your expenses or bank balance, not looking at your weight, not looking at your bank balance, not assessing your work progress, not doing medical check-ups, and procrastinating responsibilities are all strategies that keep your head in the ground. Procrastinating urgent tasks, delaying an interview with a client who is angry with you, searching for information that justifies your decision etc are examples of ostrich effect. When you realize you are falling behind and do not meet deadlines, you lose big.

Some strategies to overcome the ostrich effect and make better decisions:

The Psychology of Mind Deception

a. Take small steps

As humans we are a highly evolved species. But our brains still cannot distinguish between an unreal threat and a real one. The very thought of doing something with a bad outcome causes fear. When you have to do something uncomfortable, try to take small steps first.

b.Ask yourself powerful questions

Keep asking yourself questions. Good questions   have the power to help you make a better decision.

c. Embrace the discomfort

Many avoid discomfort and make safer choices to avoid the pain that comes from choosing an uncomfortable path. People often fail to realize that personal growth is something outside their comfort zone. Learning to embrace discomfort becomes a necessary step toward overcoming your biases and seeking out information that may be uncomfortable at first.

49. Parkinson's Law

 Parkinson's Law states that given less time to do things, more work is done. There is a proverb that says, 'No matter how much time you give to a job, the job will last for that long'. This suggests that the more time people devote to a given task, the longer it takes to complete that task. It could have been completed within that time if we had set aside less time in the first place. For example, according to Parkinson's Law, if someone is given a week to complete a task, they will often procrastinate unnecessarily even though it will actually take them only one day to complete it. So they will take that whole week to complete it.

Parkinson's Law is very important in terms of increasing productivity and predicting people's behavior at work. It is a common practice to extend the work up to the estimated time available to complete the work. Let us look at the example of a retired woman staying at home. She would sometimes spend an entire day writing and sending a postcard to her niece in Delhi. An hour would be spent finding a postcard, another looking for glasses, half an hour figuring out an address, a quarter of an hour writing, and twenty minutes deciding whether or not to take an umbrella on the way. By the time she gets to the letterbox on the next street and posts the letter, it will be too late. For a busy man, this is a matter of five minutes. Students often take a long time to complete an assignment. So whether they are given a week, a month or a semester to complete an assignment, they complete it within that time only.

The phenomenon of Parkinson's Law has been observed in many scientific studies. When given extra time to complete a task, they usually use up all that time even if they do not really need to. This will never lead to better performance at work. The most striking thing is that people often procrastinate. This can result in delaying work until just before the due date. They can never start things early.

50. Sexual Over Perception Bias

Sexual exaggeration bias is the tendency among people to overestimate the level of sexual interest in others. Men generally overestimate women's level of interest in them. On the other hand, women underestimate men's interest level. There are evolutionary reasons for this.

Chances are you have a very cocky male friend who thinks the female waiter is flirting with him when he goes to a restaurant. Every time a woman smiles at him, he jumps to lewd conclusions.

Sexual motives and interests are rarely openly expressed by people. Hence it is a subject that causes a lot of misunderstandings. Men are more likely to feel that a woman is sexually attracted to them. But women do not often think so. That is not to say that all men overestimate sexuality, nor that such overestimations do not exist among women. But it goes without saying that men are more prone to this bias than women.

Evolutionary psychologists believe that men are more likely to make this mistake because they are always trying to procreate. Males desire to mate with females solely for the purpose of increasing their reproductive potential. This is an evolutionary advantage for men.

But women are less likely to think this way because pregnancy and reproduction put more strain on a woman's body. As a result, women are more discerning, discriminating, and moderate in their mating and reproductive processes.

This bias, which mistakenly assumes that one person has a sexual interest in another, can lead to incorrect social interactions. It may lead to inappropriate or unpleasant interactions between individuals. In the context of the workplace, these misunderstandings can seriously affect future relationships between colleagues.

51. Curse of knowledge

People often say 'Knowledge is power'. But what happens if all humans are at different levels of knowledge? Have you ever noticed that if you know a lot about a subject, it is really hard to teach someone else about it?

The 'curse of knowledge' or 'curse of expertise' is a cognitive bias. We mistakenly assume that everyone knows as much as we do about a particular subject. It is difficult for us to know and guess what is the mental state of someone who does not know about the subject. That is why it is difficult for us to understand them. This is a common problem. This is called the curse of knowledge. The more you know about a subject, the harder it is to transfer that knowledge to someone with limited knowledge of that subject.

Due to the curse of knowledge, it becomes difficult for experts to teach beginners. For example, a brilliant physicist studying black holes may find it difficult to explain its basics to a high school student. Due to this phenomenon it becomes difficult to communicate with people.

For example it is difficult for a scientist to discuss their work with the general public. Often this scientist does not remember that people are not familiar with the terminology in the field of scientists. Since the curse of knowledge can cause problems in various areas of life, it is important to understand it when communicating with others.

Due to this phenomenon, people are unable to predict the behavior of others. For example, an experienced driver may be surprised to see a new driver perform a dangerous act. It is because the experienced driver does not remember that the new driver does not understand the danger of what they are doing.

The Curse of Knowledge makes it difficult for people to understand their past behavior. For example, they might have made such a bad decision based on the information they had at that time. Now they will remember that they were foolish to make that decision.

52. Magical Thinking

Magical thinking is the belief that one's ideas, thoughts, actions, words, and use of symbols can influence the course of events in the physical world. It is the assumption that there is a causal relationship between one's inner, personal experience and the external physical world. The idea that the sun, moon, wind, and rain can be influenced by one's thoughts or by some other religious practices are examples of this magical thinking. Can you win the lottery just because you want it so badly? Does it not rain because you repeatedly say it won't rain? But there are some people who think like this. Western cultures lack this magical thinking. It is the result of their industrialization, advancement of science and growth of rational thinking in those places.

We tend to feel that spirits, ghosts, patterns, and signs are everywhere, especially if we are looking for them. The human brain has a tendency to make a connection between mystical things and real life events. People believe that supernatural powers are everywhere and that we can control at least some of the things that happen in people's lives using our mental powers. It gives us a lot of comfort to think that this world is controlled by some forces that we cannot know. We would like to believe that it is possible to achieve impossible things by sheer willpower. Many motivational speakers and spiritual teachers tell us over and over again.

The Psychology of Mind Deception

Magical thinking is most common in children under the age of five, in teenagers. People often use magical thinking to gain more control over their environment and cope with the unknown.

Some people consider religion to be a form of magical thinking. But one's cultural background should also be taken into account here. To those of one religion, the beliefs of others seem like magical thinking. To an atheist, prayer itself may seem like magical thinking. Most religious people hold their beliefs as truths. So religion is not an example of magical thinking.

53. Reverse Psychology

Reverse psychology is a psychological technique used for manipulation. In order to get some desired thing from someone, instead of saying it directly, people say the opposite. Mothers use this reverse psychological strategy to get their children to eat properly. For example, the mother says to the child who does not eat all the rice, 'hey dear, you will never be able to eat all this'. Hearing this, the child eats the entire rice.

Presenting things negatively to someone is more effective than telling the matter positively. Try saying to a person who hesitates to participate in a particular sport, 'Take it from me, you won't get selected'. This will make him willing to participate in it. The father tells the stingy son that he cannot afford to buy his sister a birthday present. The brother will respond by buying her a nice gift. When the friend tells a shy friend that he is not interested in girls, he goes and talks to girls. Your partner insists they don't want a birthday present, but in reality, they want a gift from you. To surprise your partner, you buy them a gift. In fact, they were making you do that.

Let us see why reverse psychology works. When someone forces us to do something, our brain perceives it as an invasion of our intellectual freedom. So we try to reverse it and establish our independence.

It is this reverse psychology that often causes people to talk so disparagingly or negatively about themselves. For example, when someone says, 'I don't look good at all', they mean that the listener should say, 'No, you're beautiful.'

The person who comes to sell things in the house will show you very expensive things first. You won't buy anything just because they all are very expensive. Finally he shows a small cheap item. Your mind immediately rushes to buy it. In fact he came only to sell that item.

There are many examples of reverse psychology in fiction, movies, and cartoons. In William Shakespeare's play Julius Caesar, Mark Antony uses reverse psychology to incite rebellion among the townspeople. Mark Antony's praise of Brutus' actions leading to

Caesar's murder actually arouses the ire of the mob. They turn against Brutus.

54. Projection Bias

Projection bias is the error in the predictions we make about our own situation. We think that in the future too, we will be in the same state, conditions and beliefs as we are now. This results in short-sighted decision-making.

Look at these examples:

1. "I would always sleep earlier." (It will be too late after work)

2. "I never eat late." (Often you can't)

3. "I will only marry you." (You or they may have lost interest in it)

4. "I will invite you all to my wedding. Tomorrow we will drink together, eat biryani and sing songs." (Actually very few invitees will be there)

You think that you will be the same in the future as you are in the present, and that others will be in the same state of mind. But the opposite happens.

Imagine you are very hungry. You go to the supermarket and buy everything in sight. You eat some snacks before you get home and start cooking. By the time the food is cooked, you realize that you are not very hungry. Purchased foods go to waste.

Projection bias causes us to make decisions that are short-sighted and based on our current feelings, beliefs, and values. It may not last long.

External Influence (External Factors):
Things that happen outside of our control will definitely influence our decision making. We often believe that the difficulty we are experiencing now will have a long-term impact on our lives. As a result, we make important decisions like changing jobs or careers based on the present situation.

You think that you would be extremely happy for your entire life if you win the lottery. But studies have proved that lottery winners have been found to have less happiness in everyday activities compared to others.

Heat of the moment:
This is the mistake we make when we make big decisions based on our current emotional state. It may be easier for us to make rational decisions when we are calm. But in the 'hot' state i.e., when we feel intense emotions we have no idea how much those emotions influence our choices.

55. Declinism Bias

Declinism is an individual's belief that a society or institution is in decline. In particular, this perceptual error causes the past to be viewed more positively and the future more negatively. This is a way of thinking caused by cognitive biases such as rosy retrospection.

It may seem like a harmless thought, but this thought can lead you to make terrible decisions. The way we view the past, present, and future influences our beliefs and actions. Rosy retrospection makes us nostalgic. Positive memories make us happy. But they can also alter our memories to affect current decisions. One of the main problems with declinism is that it can become a self-fulfilling prophecy.

Remember the last time you heard a news story. You mostly remember the negative news. They can be about communalism, vandalism, COVID 19, climate crisis, murders, natural disasters, suicides etc. What emotions do that news make us feel? Perhaps we feel as if society is headed for an imminent destruction.

 When these images come before us, we tend to think that things are constantly getting worse. When we hear this kind of news and our parents or grandparents tell us stories about the 'good old days', we think about how great the past was. We think how good this world used to be, how the whole world is corrupt. The world is about to end, and the worst is yet to come. Alas, doomsday is approaching. The perspective that declinism brings can lead us to overly pessimistic beliefs. So it prevents us from making rational decisions to prepare for the future.

Often, we keep thinking about the deterioration of society. We blame political leaders for everything and fail to trust them. While some skepticism and resistance to the political elite can be healthy, at times the sense of hopelessness and lack of a future can leave us feeling hopeless. Also, Declinism can have a negative impact on our mental health. Remember that hope is what makes us move forward in our daily life.

56. Rosy Retrospection

Rosy retrospection refers to our tendency to remember the past more fondly than the present. This is a cognitive bias that runs parallel to the concept of nostalgia or homesickness. Nostalgia is always a biased reminder. People consider old things much better than now. The phrase is derived from the English word for 'rose-tinted glasses'.

Examples of rosy retrospection appear in various areas of life

You remember only the fun parts of a vacation you went on as a child. You remember that your college life was more fun than it actually was. You remember with strong emotions how much you enjoyed a concert you went to years ago. Our mind conveniently forgets all painful parts of our childhood, teenage days..

We often see people bemoaning the state of society today and raving about the good old days gone by. In fact, we are now passing through the best period since the world began. But whatever the current situation, people will always say that the old days were better.

For example a senior citizen watches the news on TV and says, 'Look how good the world was when I was a child. There was nothing like this then. The people were very nice. 'Now the whole world is corrupt'. But this man remembers only the good experiences of his best times, childhood and adolescence. He will not remember anything about the wars, riots, starvation, diseases and weather problems of those days.It gets worse with age. When we remember our good old days (healthy, romantic, happy) our brain filters out all the negative things and remembers only the good. This thought makes us produce happy hormones like dopamine. Thus the memories become pleasant.

A biased understanding of the past relative to the future, whether for a country or a company, can lead to incorrect assessments of both periods. When observing the progress of our company, one has a tendency to think that things were better in the past. When things are analyzed with a distorted view of the past as a reference point, the view of the present also becomes distorted. It causes the current situation to be perceived as worse than it actually is. Excessive nationalism is a by-product of this.

57. Over Justification Effect

Remember one thing we used to enjoy regularly. We suddenly lose interest in that action when we are offered some external incentives such as money or rewards for that action. Our tendency to be intrinsically motivated to engage in an activity is called the over justification effect.

Do rewards, especially financial rewards, always motivate people to do a job? On quick reflection, we think that is true. Offering gifts is the most common method used by organizations to encourage performance. For example, employees perform their best at work to get a promotion or higher income. Firms encourage such behavior by offering better bonuses or other rewards to top performers.

Incentives do not always have to be in the form of money. It comes in various forms like pride, fame, power and recognition. For example, dreams of an Olympic medal drive athletes to commit to years of relentless training. The joy of securing a high rank motivates students to prepare for the exam.

But do financial rewards always motivate people to do good? No, the truth is. In some cases, this financial reward can create a negative effect. For example, imagine you are walking down a street. You notice a blind man struggling to cross the road. Eager to help, you approach the person, take his hand and lead him to the other side. What if the blind man opens his wallet and gives you 50 rupees in return? Will you feel inspired to help other disabled people cross the road after this incident? Of course not. Because you did the deed with a good heart, without expecting any reward. So this reward will make you uncomfortable. This is called the over justification effect.

This financial reward may not hurt or affect you immediately, as in the example of helping the blind man cross the road. Often, these rewards act like a poison that destroys your motivation over time without your knowledge.

Humans are not naturally capable of recognizing what actually motivates our behavior and decisions. If asked why you work so hard, most artists don't have an answer. Similarly, many people do not have an answer to the question of why they are procrastinating on something so rewarding.

58. Third Person Effect

With the advent of electronic media, every second you hear hundreds of misleading messages that have nothing to do with the truth. But you think they would not affect you at all. In fact, many things we hear and see influence us directly and indirectly. The third-person effect is when people think that fake news and false advertising messages spread on social media have a greater impact on others than they do on themselves.

People think that good news, messages, knowledge etc will influence them more than others. The third-person effect is more pronounced when we see a news story and feel that its source is fake. News that we don't think is relevant can reinforce this third-person effect.

"I believe everything only after analyzing it very deeply in the light of my experiences and knowledge. But some people believe no matter how big the lies are". I can quickly understand politicians' lies. Some people will believe any lie. There are a lot of people who believe something which is said through a mic. But no one can make me believe things so quickly."

In fact every person thinks and believes in the above way. We do not value the arguments of people who do not agree with what we accept and believe. We believe that people who believe things we do not agree with are misguided and easily deceived.

In December 2016, the Pew Research Center conducted a survey. The question was, can you recognize fake news when you see it? Four in ten (39%) were very confident. Another 45% were somewhat confident. Only 9% were not very confident and 6% were not at all confident. Despite the fact that 84% of those surveyed were very confident in their own ability to spot fake news, 64% of those same people say that fake news causes a lot of confusion in society. In other words, the attitude produced by this third person effect is "I'm not an idiot, and others are not like me!"

59. Serial Position Effect

The serial position effect describes how the position of information in a sequence affects our memory. We remember very well the first and last items in a series. But we find it difficult to remember the items in the middle.

Suppose you make a shopping list. It has various items like vegetables, milk, cheese, eggs and toothpaste. Later, when you get to the grocery store, you realize you left your shopping list at home. You are more likely to remember the first and last items on the list, such as vegetables and toothpaste. You may have difficulty remembering other items. Of course, this does not happen in all cases, but the probability of remembering the first and last information is higher than remembering the information in the middle.

What happens when we need to remember information that we encounter only briefly? For example, suppose you are listening to a lecture in class. Your professor explains some important definitions. You start writing it down. But he speaks so fast that you cannot write it in full. So by the end of the class you will be able to remember only the first few words and the last few words.

1. Primacy effect

According to the priming effect, a person is more likely to remember the information he/she heard first, that is, the information at the top of the list. In terms of the primacy effect, information is usually stored in the individual's long-term memory.

2. Recency Effect

According to the recency effect, a person is more likely to remember what was heard last, i.e. the information at the end of the list. For example, if you learn something and tell it to be remembered later, you are more likely to remember the last piece of information. You may struggle to remember information you read first or in the middle of reading.

When one is looking to buy property or a home, the first set of options is often rejected. That is, the primary effect often does not play a significant role in real estate. Given this trend, property agents often show the best option at the end. After viewing various properties, customers' expectations get lowered. This usually makes the last option more desirable than the previously seen options. The last house seen remains in the buyer's short-term memory. Compared to the previously seen options, the buyer is likely to choose only the last option.

60. The Egocentric Bias

Egocentric bias is a cognitive bias that causes people to overestimate their own perspective when they analyze events in their lives or try to see things from other people's perspectives. Ego-centered bias causes people to either value others' points of view too far from their own, or they ignore others' points of view altogether.

For example, you commit a mistake in public. This bias can cause you to overestimate the likelihood that others will notice. Because you will feel that others are focusing on your activities as much as you are.

When you give a public speech, you assume that your stage fright is more obvious to others than it really is. You overestimate the amount of things you've contributed to a group project. You may believe that all your colleagues share the same political beliefs and social values as you. Although it is true that you played a relatively minor role in a past event, you may be reminding yourself that you played a major role in it.

People with this bias tend to think that they are better than average in terms of intelligence, compassion, beauty, and other abilities. Most people would rate themselves as better than average drivers. A person with an egocentric bias thinks that it is less likely that he will die in a car accident or that he will get cancer.

All of these examples have one thing in common. People tend to rely too much on their own perspective. That is, in many cases, egocentric bias causes people to attribute their beliefs, desires, thoughts, and feelings to others. This happens especially when these people are in close contact with others. It interferes with people's ability to empathize because it causes you to focus primarily on your own feelings and ignore how other people feel.

There are many subcategories of this egocentric bias. The illusion of transparency, the spotlight effect, the false consensus effect, the curse of knowledge etc.

61. The Illusion of Transparency

This bias causes others to believe that a person's thoughts and feelings are more understandable than they actually are. This is primarily due to the self-centered bias. As we are quick to understand our inner state, we think that others will also be quick to understand our state of mind.

Many people struggle in life due to the illusion of transparency. People think that everyone else can clearly understand their sadness, emotions, and frustrations. They believe that the rest of us can immediately guess what their needs are. But people are not always open books. So if you really need something, the only option you have is to say it openly or ask for it verbally.

The Psychology of Mind Deception

Liars tend to overestimate that others can detect their lies very well. People who experience emotional distress feel that their distress is very obvious to others. People who eat something that tastes bad assume that their disgust is more obvious to bystanders than it actually is.

Suppose, you are giving a speech in front of a large group of people. You are really stressed. You think your audience understands your stress so well that they notice every quiver in your voice and every little mistake in your speech. The truth is, the audience doesn't care about little things like this. No matter how good you are at reading other people's emotions, it is impossible to truly understand another person's emotional state. When trying to empathize with others, it is better to say, 'Your state of mind is beyond my comprehension' than saying 'I can understand what you are going through."

62. The Spotlight Effect

We go to a social gathering well dressed up. Our perception is that everyone will notice us. We assume that our behavior, dress, and small flaws will be noticed and understood by the rest of the group.. In fact, other people will only notice your shortcomings if someone else point them out.

Let us say you spill some water at a party, your clothes get a little torn, or a bit of curry falls on your body. In fact you will become very conscious and upset about these small mistakes. You will think that everyone is paying attention to you. In reality very few people notice this and most people don't think much of it.

Just like that, you get very thin or you buy a new pair of shoes. When you enter a gathering you expect others to notice exactly this and tell you about it.

When you get on a stage to preach or when you go out with your boyfriend for the first time, you think everyone is paying attention because you are the center of attention in your world. In fact no one really cares about anyone else because every person is in the same state of mind.

Every public speaker thinks that he is making some great contribution to society and that the people listening will remember that speech forever. But in reality very few people listen to the whole speech.

The spotlight effect creates the feeling that the people around us have an exaggerated view of our own importance. This causes us to misjudge situations and make decisions based on feelings that come from over thinking that we are being watched.

Believing that others are always watching out for us can be detrimental to our mental health. We always try to do our actions for the sake of others. If we continually fall into the trap of the spotlight effect, we may waste many good opportunities based on the false assumption that others are always analyzing us. The spotlight effect can also cause social anxiety, which can harm a person's physical and mental health.

63. Survivorship Bias

Survival bias is a common perceptual error that distorts our understanding of the world. Every day we hear the stories of many successful people. But we don't pay enough attention to the past failures of these same successful people.

For every great success in the world, there are thousands of failures to tell. But stories of failures are not as compelling as stories of success. So they are rarely spoken or written. As we repeat every success story, we forget the real statistics of success and failure and overestimate the chances of success in life.

Let's look at one of the most famous examples of survivorship bias. It was the time of World War II. At that time, the US military asked the great mathematician Abraham Wald to study how to protect aircrafts from being shot down. What they were initially doing was inspecting the aircrafts returning from combat without major injuries, analyzing where they were hit the worst, and then reinforcing those areas.

However, Wald realized that they were making a big mistake in their analysis falling victim to survivorship bias. In reality they were supposed to be inspecting crashed planes. Why it broke was to be analyzed.

This misconception is most often used by motivational gurus and self-help books. When we only focus on successful people in life, we suffer from survivorship bias. Often our attention is drawn to people who take risks and succeed despite problems.

For example we might have heard it many times that many of today's billionaires including Bill Gates and Mark Zuckerberg did not complete their university studies. Yet they have achieved success. This information attracted considerable media attention. The New York Times later reported that the number of young people who decided not to go to university increased a lot after this.

In 2011,a Silicon Valley entrepreneur Peter Theil launched a new program. He promised an award of $100,000 to young entrepreneurs who want to drop out of school and start a new business. The future of many people has been ruined only because of this. No one bothered to report the information of thousands of people who dropped out of university and became a huge failure in life. It is not newsworthy.

64. Telescopic Effect

The telescoping effect refers to our inaccurate perceptions of time. People remember recent events as if they happened long ago (backward telescoping). But things that happened in the past are remembered as happening in the recent past (forward telescoping). This misunderstanding in memory can occur whenever we make assumptions about past events.

As we age, this misunderstanding increases. It is easy for us to remember something beautiful (like a concert we really liked). We would think, 'That happened not long ago'. In fact, it may have happened years or even decades ago. When we think about something dramatic (like an illness or accident) that happened a year or two ago, we're like, 'Oh that was so long ago.' It's a trick of the mind to revel in pleasant memories and minimize unpleasant ones.

Every year on September 11th, people can be heard commenting that the day of the terrorist attacks in New York was not so long ago. And people are surprised when they hear the media say the number of years that have actually passed since the disaster. Conversely, a few months into the COVID-19 pandemic, we may feel like a lot of time has passed. However, incidents of forward telescoping, such as 9/11, are more common than backward telescoping.

While it is easy for us to spot these memory lapses in others, it is not always easy to spot them in ourselves.

65. The Bias Blind Spot

In this cognitive bias each person thinks they are less prone to bias than others.

For example, people think that other people's political positions are bias-blind and that they are influenced by various biases. At the same time we assume that our own political positions are perfectly rational. The bias blind spot can strongly affect anyone in a variety of areas. So it is important to understand this.

Generally, people want to have objective and accurate opinions. At the same time, external factors such as limited information, strong emotions, and self-interest can all lead us to adopt opinions that are not objective, accurate, or inaccurate. In general, people are good at recognizing the effects of different biases on other people.

Suppose a person regularly buys ice cream of a particular company. We don't think he does it because he likes the taste of it. Instead we assume that he was influenced by that company's advertising. But even if we are influenced by the same company and buy the same ice cream, we will not accept that it is the influence of advertising.

The Psychology of Mind Deception

In the US, most citizens advocate gun control. People are convinced that more guns lead to more violence. On the other hand, these same people buy guns to protect themselves. They think they are unsafe without guns. We always make a decision and interpret it using data to justify it.

When doctors receive gifts from pharmaceutical companies, they tell others that the gifts do not affect their decisions about which drugs to prescribe. They don't think this bias will make them prescribe that particular company's drug. However, other physicians will exclaim that they are biased in the pressure of these gifts. Meanwhile they will continue to believe that their own decisions are not.

Bias blind spots can sometimes influence people's view of other people. This can cause people to underestimate the potential for bias by people we consider to be experts we respect. For example, people who think favorably of police officers, financial advisors, priests, or doctors may not even consider that they too may be biased.

66. Illusory Superiority

Here people feel a false sense of superiority. This bias causes people to overestimate their own qualities and abilities and underestimate their shortcomings compared to others.

From the early days of the field of psychology to the present, the prevailing thought in society is that we have low confidence in our abilities. It is a common thought in society that inferiority complex, self-loathing and lack of appreciation of one's own abilities affect every human being. But over the past 50 years, studies by social psychologists in various societies have proven this notion wrong.

Studies have shown that nearly 90% of drivers self-declare that they are above average.87% of MBA students consider themselves to be performing better than their peers. 94% of professors think they are well above average. About 70% of high school seniors say they have above average leadership skills. But only 2% say they are below average. People think that they are less likely to get a corona infection. You might have noticed most people saying that their Facebook posts are of above average standard.

When people are incompetent they jump to wrong conclusions and make unfortunate choices. The incompetence to recognize their own mistakes is yet another big problem here. Incompetent people insist that their ways are right instead of dwelling on their wrong ways. As Charles Darwin said, ignorance more frequently begets confidence than does knowledge: it is those who know little, and not those who know much, who so positively assert that this or that problem will never be solved by science.

The Psychology of Mind Deception

It is quite dangerous to lack a sense of reality about one's own personality beyond an average level. We are often unaware of how our attitudes are affecting other people and these attitudes can have a profound effect on their lives and the lives of others.

As we get older, we tend to attribute these past failures to others. We think in this direction in the study of identification with other persons and in self-examination. We become convinced that we are more capable than our friends, fairer than our friends, more handsome than the average, less prejudiced, better drivers than others, better sons, more thoughtful, younger than others, and more lively than others.

If you're reading this and think I don't belong in this group, it means your self-perception is not quite right. Each person assumes that the characteristics that a general statistic says do not apply to them. In short, no one thinks they are just an average person.

67. Response Bias

Response bias refers to our tendency to give inaccurate or incorrect answers to questions in surveys, structured interviews, or self-administered psychological questionnaires. This bias can be intentional or accidental. But these biased responses make survey data useless. This may become a particular problem in self-reporting surveys.

For example, suppose a researcher studying drinking on college campuses conducts a survey at a college. In this context, a key concern is to ensure that the survey is unbiased and non-discriminatory. Respondents are more likely to underestimate their drinking if they see survey results skewing toward blaming heavy drinking. This may lead to biased survey results.

When this bias occurs, people come up with answers based on external factors such as social norms or what the researcher wants to hear. We lose the opportunity to self-analyze and think about how the research topic is really relevant to us. As for the researcher, he gets inaccurate data.

a. Social response bias

This is also known as social desirability bias. As a result, respondents often over report good behaviors and underreport bad behaviors.

Here are some things that may be misreported:

1. Strengths and weaknesses

2. Personality

3. Sexual behavior

4. Religion and Spirituality

5. Financial income

The Psychology of Mind Deception

6. Unlawful conduct

7. To appear more socially desirable, respondents will answer this way. E.g. High salary.

If survey respondents are asked about their social, educational and economic status they give inflated responses.

b. Order effects

Response bias may occur due to the order of questions, reason, etc. For example, if you ask employees to discuss problems with their line manager in detail before asking them how happy they are with their jobs, their answer to the second question will influence their response to the first. If you change the order of those questions, their answers may change.

c. Recency bias

Recency bias affects those who select the last read answer.

d. Hostile bias

Asking respondents about unpleasant memories or negative experiences can make them uncomfortable. Examples of this are questions related to divorce, debt, and death.

e. Non-differentiation (straight lining)

Some people have difficulty distinguishing between the choices given in the answer. In these cases, they may give the same answer or similar responses to all questions using the same scale.

f. Neutral Answer Choices

This is the way some people consistently choose neutral answer options. These include options like 'Don't Know', 'N/A' and 'No Comment'.

g. Extremely responsive

This mostly affects survey questions where options like "Strongly Agree" and "Strongly Disagree" are available. Respondents may select extreme answer options for each scale.

68. Control Bias

Control bias refers to our tendency to overestimate the degree of control we have over our emotional behaviors. We think we have a lot of control over our "internal urges" such as hunger, drug addiction, fatigue, or sexual arousal.

The Kellogg School of Management in Chicago conducted a study on "control bias." They found that as independent individuals we have no idea how much temptation we can withstand. The study found that people who were less confident about their ability to resist temptation performed better in a test to resist temptation. They did it because they kept the source of temptation as far away as possible.

Imagine you are a university student preparing for final year exams. You make a schedule to study for the exam. You decide to sit and study in the library for consecutive nights in order to get good marks for the exam. But after a day you start feeling tired. But you are an experienced student and have a good ability to endure fatigue. But after a few days you feel very tired one afternoon. All you can think about is going home and sleeping. Finally you leave the library and get home and oversleep. You have controlled your mental and physical urge to relax. You tried to minimize the effects of fatigue. This thought process has led you to create a poor study plan. And finally the whole plan goes awry and you fail to prepare adequately for the exams.

Most of us have gone through the situations described above in one way or another. After watching a documentary, we vow to avoid fried foods. But then we may not be able to resist when we see good oil sweets in the tea shop. Or we may be a frequent smoker. But we believe that we can easily give it up anytime. But most of the time we would not be able to resist this temptation. This exaggerated view of our own composure can lead to poor decision-making and putting ourselves in situations where our composure is tested. So is our conception of sex. The truth is that we have far less control over sex than we think.

69. The Bystander Effect-The indifferent spectator

Suppose an accident happens right in front of your eyes. You would certainly take some action to help the injured person, right?

Although we'd all like to believe this is true, psychologists say that deciding whether or not you want to get involved depends on how many other people are present there.

Let's look at two incidents reported by the New York Police Department:

Following the infamous murder of Catherine Genovese in New York City in 1964, social psychologists Bib Latane and John Darley introduced the concept of the bystander effect. Many saw a young woman named Catherine Genovese being chased by an assailant as she came home from work at three in the morning. He assaults this woman. But she didn't die. Unfortunately, the assailant returned moments later and stabbed Catherine Genovese to death. Despite Genovese's repeated calls for help, none of the dozen or so people in a nearby apartment building who heard her cries called police to report the incident. The attack first began at 3:20 a.m., but it wasn't until 3:50 a.m. that someone first called the police. It took only two minutes for the police to arrive,but she was dead by that time.

In New York City's busiest Central Park parade (central park parade), a group of young men were seen harassing about sixty women. Thousands of people were watching it. But not a single person tried to call and inform the police. The villain here is the bystander effect. Everyone thought that with so many people there, someone would have alerted the police by then. Each person will remain silent in the hope that someone else will respond even if they see an incident in front of them that needs to be responded to. Nowadays people will record such incidents on their mobile phone and post on social media.

 The sad truth is that even if many people see a person lying in a car accident on a very busy road, no one will be ready to take them to the hospital. Often this is due to the thought that "someone else will help him". On the other hand, in a desolate place, the chances of a victim of an accident getting help are slightly higher. It is just that he would not be noticed until someone sees him.

 Social psychologists who study the bystander effect say that the more the number of people who are present when an event occurs, the less likely someone is to respond.

When an emergency occurs, the first decision a person must make is to analyze whether there really is a problem. When a person is alone, this decision is made based on past experience and training. However, Lathan and Darley state that in the presence of others, individuals tend to look to others for the right decision. The indifference of others can cause a delay or failure to take action.

The second decision a person must make in the event of an emergency is to take appropriate action. Each person in a large group may feel that it is not their responsibility to act first. But every person should think that I will act even if no one acts.

70. Salience Bias

Salience bias refers to our tendency to completely ignore things that do not grab our attention and focus more on items or information that gets our attention.

Imagine that while watching the news on TV, your attention is drawn to the news of some attack in the city. Nothing increases your risk of becoming a victim of violence. But the memory of the violence in the city lingers in your mind. It will make you more nervous when you leave the house.

The sanitation department at Schiphol Airport in Amsterdam was constantly faced with a problem. No matter how many times a day they clean, men's urinals are always dirty. As we all know men often lack 'urination precision'. Public urinals become unsanitary as hundreds of people urinate in such an imprecise manner. The cleaning process is expensive in Europe. Schiphol Airport has solved their problem with a simple but brilliant solution. How?

They drew a picture of a fly on each bowl to urinate on. It looked like a real fly. These little carvings were incredibly effective. People were trying to urinate on exactly this fly. Thus the flies reduced urine leakage by 80% and reduced total cleaning costs by 8%.

"Boys are simple-minded and like to play with their urine, so if there's something in the toilet bowl, they'll urinate precisely on it,"
The Psychology of Mind Deception

said a member of the team that invented the solution. This is a behavioral phenomenon known as salience bias.

71. Implicit Bias

We all have biases. Implicit biases are assumptions we unconsciously make about people or groups. This is also known as unconscious bias. People unconsciously hold this implicit bias based on a variety of factors, such as age, socioeconomic status, weight, gender, race, or sexual orientation. We judge others based on this. These biases are not always negative. It is shaped by a survival instinct. It helps us associate with people we perceive to be similar to ourselves because it is considered more 'safe'.

There are examples of unconscious biases throughout our personal and professional lives. In his book Blink: The Power of Thinking Without Thinking, Malcolm Gladwell notes that about 3.9% of adult males in the general population are 6 feet 2 inches or taller. However, he found that about one-third, or 33.3%, of a random sample of CEOs fell into this group.

According to Gladwell, this can be related to the unconscious belief that height is associated with success. A 2020 Chinese study corroborates this hypothesis.. They found that each taller-than-average officer had 10% to 13% of their annual income in salary over others.

In 2018, two black men walked into a Starbucks in Philadelphia to attend a business meeting. The manager asked them to leave. They refused to leave saying they were waiting for their partner. The manager called the police and the police arrived and arrested them. In post-arrest interviews, these black men said they believed the manager treated them this way because of their race. Starbucks immediately decided to conduct company-wide training to combat this apparent unconscious bias and prevent conscious discrimination.

A manager only assigns work that requires technical excellence to younger people based on the assumption that younger staff members are better at technology. Unconscious bias can also occur in the classroom.

Examples:

Affinity Bias: The tendency of individuals to be attracted to people who are similar to themselves.

Beauty Bias: Individuals' tendency to treat attractive people more favorably.

Name bias: The tendency for individuals to judge someone based on their name. This can even adversely affect the hiring processes of companies.

Body weight Bias: The tendency to judge or think negatively about individuals who are overweight or underweight.

The Psychology of Mind Deception

Unconscious bias can take the form of race-ethnicity bias, age bias, gender bias (LGBTQIA+ community bias), ability bias, and more.

72. Social Norms Bias

Social norm bias refers to collective beliefs about what kind of behavior is appropriate in a particular situation. These behaviors can be formed from specific rituals to cultures. For example, these range from the Western custom of shaking hands when you meet someone for the first time to general rules that govern your behavior in public and influence our perception of others.

Suppose you buy and drink tea from a shop on a busy street. When you see everyone throwing their paper cups on the road after drinking tea, you will do the same even if there is a waste bin nearby.

There is a strange custom that I see in Mysore. They keep honking along with the accelerator to move the vehicle forward. At 1:00 or 2:00 in the night, they keep honking even if there is no vehicle or person on the road within a kilometer radius. My observation is that nine out of ten people do this. This could be a habit that would have been emulated from a single perverted person.

The Psychology of Rituals

Metha was a man who became rich through his own efforts. He was very fond of kittens. Kittens roamed freely in his workplace and home.

But gradually these kittens often started disturbing him at work. He got rid of almost all kittens except one. In the end there was only a kitten that remained in his house. At the end of the month when the money is being counted, this kitten comes in and lays out all the money. When this became a big nuisance, he did one thing. The kitten was placed in a small cage before the counting began. Then he will bring it to him. When the cat starts fussing, he will occasionally give some biscuits. His children and grandchildren grew up watching these works.

Years passed. Metha was dead. His sons and sons-in-law also expanded his business empire. Now they have machines to count the currency notes. The accounts are looked at by a computer and a chartered accountant. But they followed the ritual that blessed Metha. Before the audit, they started keeping a kitten in a cage and gave it a biscuit every ten minutes. The business was progressing well.

Our tendency to follow social norms in certain situations can lead us to behave in harmful ways. Sometimes we would be forced to remain silent at times when we are supposed to respond. When we

The Psychology of Mind Deception

see that the majority agree on something, even if there are opposing opinions, we tend to accept it or remain silent. You don't even consider the possibility that many people have the same opposing opinions as you. Swimming against the current is difficult.

73. Selective Perception

Selective perception is the process of picking out and accepting only those things from a speech, book, or speech that they feel are true. We take only what we need, completely ignoring opposing views. In other words, a person sees only what a person wants to see in an image. No one sees the real picture.

Perception

Suppose two people see the same thing at the same time. Even if the visual signals that fall on their eyes are the same, their analysis will be of two types. This is called perception. Individuals' attitudes, life circumstances, interests, repressed emotions, social, educational, and cultural circumstances etc will all significantly influence their perceptions. Things that do not come under the scope of our desires, interests, etc would be peeled away. Selective perception is when we pick up only a few sentences that we want from an ocean of information.

This perceptual bias causes people to see only what they want in news and advertisements in the media. All people tend to 'see things' based on their own particular frame of reference. We interpret all information only in ways that are consistent with our existing values and beliefs. As discussed earlier this is called confirmation bias. Psychologists say that this process happens unconsciously.

Let's look at an interesting example;

On the occasion of a bishop's visit to the seminary, he gave a speech to its clergy students. While talking about the glory of motherhood, he quoted a quote by Pandit Nehru: "Our first prime minister, Pandit Jawaharlal Nehru, once said, "I have felt the greatest satisfaction when I slept on the lap of someone else's wife. That woman was none other than my own father's wife. I got the greatest solace of my life on my mother's lap.

It was the seminary students in their late adolescence and early youth who were listening to this speech. One of them got an opportunity to preach in a parish after two weeks. This is how he quoted the lines from the speech of the Bishop at the Seminary.

"I will tell you the truth, my dear parishioners. The greatest satisfaction I ever had was when I slept on the lap of another man's wife.".In fact during the Bishop's speech this clergy student did not pay much attention to the things before and after this sentence.

The believers were disturbed when they heard this sentence. When he saw that things were getting worse, the aspirant priest said, "Don't be upset by this. Not only I, but our bishop also has done the same.

This selective attention and rejection occurs most frequently in analyzes of religious texts. Finding answers to any problems in life from religious books is also based on this same flawed judgment. When a text is taken from a religious book to analyze a current situation, people forget the era, circumstances or language in which it was written. People twist sentences to make that fit anywhere they need.

74. Status Quo Bias

Status quo bias is defined as our tendency to remain in the status quo and our resistance to any change. Change is a scary thing for many people. Maybe that's why many people prefer to stay in their comfort zone. In psychology, this tendency is called status quo bias. When changes occur, people perceive them as a loss or disadvantage.

Status quo bias is often associated with other cognitive biases.

Choice Paralysis: It can be overwhelming for people when there are so many options to choose from. So they decide to stay in the status quo.

Loss Aversion: The losses we face by moving away from the status quo and doing something different discourage us from making a decision. As a result, people generally prefer to stick with what they know if it is satisfactory.

Sunk Cost Fallacy: If a person has invested a lot of time, money, or effort in a particular endeavor, they will stick with it no matter how much loss they later realize.

Status quo bias can have a serious impact on everyday decisions. For example, have you found yourself ordering the same menu item every time you visit your favorite restaurant? It is not because you are not tempted by some of the new items on the menu. But you are reluctant to take the risk of ordering something and facing a challenge.

When making decisions, we avoid mental difficulties so much that we arrive at a quick decision. People's preference for the default option can have significant consequences. For example, when visiting a hospital, people have to register separately to become organ donors. People will avoid even this minor difficulty. As a result very few people register as organ donors and a very few lives are saved.

Some experts believe that understanding our biases can help us change our daily behavior. But Nobel Laureate Daniel Kahneman says it is impossible for humans to avoid bias.

The Psychology of Mind Deception

75. Source Confusion

Also known as source confusion and source misattribution. This is a type of memory error. Not being able to remember where certain information or memories come from.

One day in London, a psychologist was brought to the police station accused of rape. The woman who accused him of raping had seen this psychologist on television before she was raped. The young woman suddenly switched between the face of the assailant and the face of the psychologist. The woman was unable to distinguish where she saw these two faces (Schacter, 1999). This is an example of cognitive bias called source confusion.

The attributes and credibility we give to our memory are completely unrealistic. Memory is not something that captures things like a digital recorder, preserves them in perfect perfection, and retrieves them without a scratch. Our memory is just a collection of images, information and feelings scattered here and there. This information may be revised from time to time. Our experiences, our mental, physical, and health conditions, our belief systems, education, culture, etc. all influence the rewriting of these memory sequences.

You see a post on Twitter or Instagram. But you remember that you saw it on TV. One of the most basic forms of misattribution is source confusion. When people cannot recall information correctly, it turns to the wrong source. We may be confused about where we saw a face or read an article. As a result of this eyewitness accounts are often falsely accused.

Cryptomnesia

One fine morning something that you had completely forgotten suddenly comes back to your memory. But this is not remembered as a thing of the past. Instead it is experienced as something new with all its freshness and emotions. Sometimes this will be remembered as your complete creativity or imagination. It is estimated that many plagiarism happens in this way. People will completely forget something they have read or heard in the past and it will appear to them as a new creation in their minds years later.

Carl Gustav Jung, a prominent early psychologist, cites the best example of cryptomnesia from a book by Friedrich Nietzsche. There is an incident described in the book 'Thus Spoke Zarathustra'. Nietzsche suddenly forgot the contents of a book he had read in the past and years later he remembered and wrote it down as a work of his own imagination. It was accused of plagiarism.

Lord Byron, JM Barrie, Helen Keller ,RL Stevenson etc are believed to have suffered from this amnesia. In many of their works, events and characters from books she read and many others wrote appear as they are. They did not steal those knowingly.

76. Suggestibility

Suggestibility refers to how likely we are to change our behavior based on the suggestions of others. This bias often leads to false eyewitness testimony.

Suggestibility in psychology refers to the brain's tendency to fill in gaps in our memory with information provided by others. Often it plants false memories. People are more prone to suggestion when experiencing intense emotions.

We tend to act or take instructions based on information provided by others. People's self-esteem, their age, the circumstances in which they were raised, and their determination all affect the extent to which they will accept and act on suggestions.

Children have a greater tendency than adults to accept information without analyzing it. This suggestibility can be seen in all their actions. A good example of suggestibility found in our daily life is yawning. If a person is seen yawning, one can see people around him doing the same one after the other. This is an unconscious suggestion.

For example, you go to a dentist. You experience mild difficulties there. But another person later told you how horrible this dentist's approach was. Based on this discussion, we misremember the experience at that dentist's clinic as horrible. We avoid seeing him later.

It has been said that memories are rewritten in the human brain without our knowledge. But it is possible to consciously add to one's memory events that never happened. This has been proven in psychosocial experiments conducted at the University of Washington in the United States. In the same way, in psychotherapy, hypnosis, lie tests like polygraph, narco analysis memories are planted. People's memories travel in different directions according to the instructions of other people.

According to Dr. Elizabeth Tofu (University of Washington, USA), one of the most studied researchers in this field, our memory is like Wikipedia. Once we have copied information, we and others rewrite it. If it is used effectively, some bad habits can be removed from children.

77. Self-Serving Bias

This is the belief that the positive events and successes that occur in our lives are the result of our own character, abilities or actions. At the same time, we blame our failures on external factors unrelated to our nature. This is a common cognitive bias that has fascinated researchers globally for decades. Age, culture, and psychological issues can also contribute to this bias.

The Psychology of Mind Deception

When we get a good grade in an exam, we attribute success to our own abilities. But when we get a bad grade, we blame external factors. These external factors can be things like the professors inability to teach the subject, the difficulty of the subject, or the mistakes of the group members.

This seemingly harmless habit can have significant effects on our lives as we age. Hence it is very necessary to identify and reduce such related behavior.

When there is a car accident, drivers blame each other. No one even thinks they've made a mistake. Every person thinks that if their team wins in a basketball game, it is because of their ability.

Control point

Locus of Control (LOC) – describes the causes of events in life and the justifications a person gives for them. LOC has two categories, internal and external.

A person with internal LOC will believe that their success is the result of their own hard work, effort, and perseverance. Individuals with extrinsic LOC tend to attribute their successes to external factors such as luck, help from others, timing, and God's blessing. Individuals with an internal LOC are more likely to show a self-serving bias, especially in relation to achievement. Self-serving biases can affect communities and nations as a whole.

Take a look at a study conducted by researchers at Carnegie Mellon University. They examined citizens' perceptions of which countries should reduce carbon emissions. They conducted these surveys among college students in China and the United States. The researchers noted that each group of students held self-serving biases when it came to the financial burdens of climate change mitigation and reducing greenhouse gas emissions. Both countries believed that their country was not to blame and that their actions were spotless.

The positive side of self-serving bias

One benefit of this bias is that it makes people persevere even in the face of adversity. An unemployed person may believe that the weak economy is the cause of their unemployment and seek employment again. But if a person thinks that he cannot get a job because of his incompetence, he will never try for a job. As a result he will remain unemployed forever. If an athlete can believe that his failure in a previous event was a result of bad weather rather than a lack of skill, he will be more motivated to perform well.

78. The Law of the Instrument

The Law of the Instrument is a cognitive bias that involves overreliance on a familiar tool. It is also known as Maslow's hammer/or golden hammer. As the world famous American psychologist Abraham Maslow said, "If the only tool you have is a hammer, then everything you see will be like a nail."

The Law of the Instrument can make us ineffective. When trying to solve a problem or complete a task, we tend to stick to using only a particular skill or tool that we are familiar with. A lot of energy and time are wasted trying to solve a problem or work in only one systematic way. When we acknowledge the fact that using the same skill or tool over and over again makes us more proficient in its use, it can prevent us from acquiring other skills.

A major concern with the law of instrument is its presence within the educational system. All children are gifted. But each has its own strengths and weaknesses. The idea that they can all learn the same things at the same phase and in the same way is illogical. But this is the way education is done in our country. Our teachers do not understand that every student has different abilities and not everyone can learn everything. If we apply this logic we could say that an elephant is worse than a monkey just because it cannot climb trees.

Déformation professionnelle

"Deformation professionnelle" is a French term. It is a cognitive bias that causes people to view the world only through the perspective of one's occupation. Take a college late night party for example. Let us see how people in various fields evaluate this party. A doctor is concerned about the long-term effects of heavy drinking on students' livers. They may also be concerned about the risk of sexually transmitted diseases. On the other hand, a psychologist only talks about the mental disorders that substance abuse causes in students. Finally, a police officer will talk about the nuisance the party will cause to the neighbors.

Deformation can lead to professional bias when people with expertise in a particular field try to generalize their skills to other contexts. Thinking like a physicist can be challenging for a doctor and vice versa. This is because they all face very different problems in their workplace. For companies or laboratories that require a wide range of skills, it is useful to hire people with expertise in many areas.

The Einstellung effect

Another bias that can be caused by instrumental law is the Einstellung effect. This is the tendency to see our past experiences as a solution to all problems. This is a person's predisposition to solve a given problem in a specific manner even though better or more appropriate methods of solving the problem exist.

79. Representation Heuristic

As we know by now heuristics are the mental shortcuts we take to make decisions. When we are trying to make a decision and are faced with uncertainty, we often rely on a specific mental shortcut known as the representation heuristic. We make decisions by comparing the current situation with the ideas already set in our mind.

Although these shortcuts can speed up the decision-making process, they can lead to poor choices and stereotypes. We do not necessarily have the time or resources to compare all the information before every decision and every choice. So these heuristics help us reach decisions quickly and efficiently. Sometimes these mental shortcuts can be helpful. But in other cases, they can lead to errors or cognitive biases.

Let's see some examples:
Suppose you are going to the cinema with your friend Meera. She has also invited two other friends of hers. You are seeing them for the first time. Meera had said that one of them is a mathematician and the other is a musician. Finally you meet Meera's friends John and Thrun. John is a shy guy who wears glasses. He wears loose old fashioned clothes. But Tharun is a fashionable man in a t-shirt, jeans and sunglasses. In this scenario you immediately assume that John will be the mathematician and Tharun will be the musician. In fact, the opposite was true. Let's look at some other examples of this bias.

Consumers tend to assume that a product in a store is of relatively high quality if its packaging is designed to resemble a high-end brand. People think that very cold winters indicate a lack of global warming. Gamblers choose lottery tickets with seemingly random numbers. Investors may be interested in buying a stock that has recently shown an unusually high rate of return.

Heuristics can also affect the decisions people make in the workplace. For example, in one study they conducted, researchers found that managers in organizations made biased decisions more than 50% of the time. The problem here is taking heuristic or shortcuts in decisions.

Social Relations: This representation heuristic affects the decisions we make when meeting new people. This heuristic can play a role in how people vote in political elections and the candidates they support. For example, people have an image in their minds of what a good leader should be. They will vote for those who fit that mental image. They do not bother to research their background.

Judges often pass sentences only by comparing the appearance of the accused with the picture of the criminal in their mind. Clinicians may make treatment decisions based on how closely a patient and their symptoms match an existing prototype. For example, we might think of a farmer as a hard-working innocent man. Conversely, we tend to think of a librarian as calm, polite, and soft-spoken. In fact, this is not always the case.

The Psychology of Mind Deception

80. Consistency Bias

"I am the same person. My convictions, opinions and thoughts have not changed. My personality has always been the same."
Those are the refrains we hear regularly. The term 'consistency bias' was first coined by Dr.Anthony Greenwald, a professor at the University of Washington. Consistency bias is the phenomenon that makes you think that you have held the same opinion about something in the past. Whether you know it or not, admit it or not, your opinions have changed according to the circumstances of each time. When a person says that he has never changed it is completely ridiculous. Whether you admit it ot not change is a constant thing,

Our mind and memory remember good things and repress negative events. Memories are constantly reconstructed to make the past more compatible with the present. This reconstruction gives relevance to our current attitudes and beliefs.

An experiment was conducted in the USA in 1965 to find out how much political opinion among young people changes. A group of students and politicians were asked to record their opinions about organizations, leaders and political ideas. Eight years later they asked the same questions and asked to record their opinions.

After that, they were asked what their opinion was about the same things eight years ago? The majority said that their opinion was the same then too. Only 30 percent of people remembered what their opinion was in the past. But there have been many changes between the opinion they recorded eight years ago and the current opinion.

You are actually a different person every year. Sometimes your opinions can change drastically in just two weeks. Only by keeping a diary will you realize that you're past opinions and desires are so far from the present.

81. Social Loafing

Social loafing refers to the tendency of people to do the least amount of work when they are part of a group. When there is a situation where everyone in the group must work together to achieve a common goal, each person will try to do the least amount of work. Meanwhile, if each member of the group is given personal responsibility, they will do more work.

There is a general belief that a difficult task or project can be accomplished by bringing together a large number of people. People generally have a perception that each individual will work harder in a collective effort. But in reality we will try to do the least amount of work, knowing that each individual will not receive personal recognition in a collective action. There is a saying that everyone's responsibility is nobody's responsibility.

The Psychology of Mind Deception

Social loafing has negative consequences for the group and the individuals in the group. When some individuals in the group contribute too little, it affects the group dynamics. This can split the group and affect collective group functioning. For example, if only five of the eight members of a team do most of the work, it often creates an 'in' group (members who work hard) and an 'out' group (members who don't contribute). It can result in resentment to grow easily between the two factions. This results in lower productivity than a homogeneous group. There is also more emotional stress here for those who do all the work.

In 1974, psychologist Alan Ingram conducted a social experiment. A man was blindfolded and the end of a large rope was handed to him. It was a device in which a section of this rope was attached to a machine and pulled from one side to form a resistance. (This gave the impression of a lot of people to pull there.) After being blindfolded, Alan tells him that this is a tug-of-war and that he has a few more people on his side.

In the next round of tug-of-war, the same man was told that he had no one with him and that he would have to compete against the other side alone. Alan Ingram documented the labor of people in both these phases. He found that each person worked up to 18 percent harder when they thought they were alone.

This is also called the Ringerman effect. The French engineer Maximilian Ringermann assigned a few men individually and in groups to pull a strain gauge invented by him by his experiments. In this experiment too the labor of each individual in collective labor was much less than the sum of individual labor.

Sports psychologists have long warned against this behavior. Therefore, in the final training session before each game, the individual performance of each player is captured by a different camera and shown to them. This is to remove the social loafing thought from the players that no matter how they play, there is no problem.

This includes 360 degree evaluation which measures the work performance, hard work, sincerity, perseverance, honesty and punctuality of every worker and officer.

82. Florence Nightingale effect

The Florence Nightingale effect is the phenomenon in which another person who cares for a person feels romantic feelings for the person being cared for. More specifically, Florence Nightingale Syndrome is a psychological complication. When caring for a vulnerable patient. Here caregivers may develop romantic and often sexual feelings toward the patient. In turn, the patient too may feel the same love for their caregivers. It is because they see this nurse as their protector.

Origin

This effect is named after Florence Nightingale, a pioneer in the field of nursing in the second half of the 19th century. She was so dedicated to the patients and their care that she would go out at night to see the sick with a lamp like no one had done before. Her work earned her the nickname "The Lady with the Lamp". Nightingale is considered by many to be the founder of modern nursing. She never fell in love with the patients. Many people loved them. But she didn't even get married, fearing that it would be a challenge to his work.

Florence Nightingale Syndrome is not a medically recognized disease. It is just something that's used in popular psychology, movies, and more. The effects of Florence Nightingale syndrome can affect both the patient and the caregiver. It is wrong for a person to feel harmless love for another person. But when that feeling leads them to other undesirable actions, problems arise.

83. The Rashomon effect

The Rashomon effect is situations in which people who have seen the same event give conflicting interpretations or descriptions of it. It is a method of storytelling and writing used in film to give different perspectives on the same event. The effect is named after Japanese movie director Akira Kurosawa's 1950 film Rashomon. It is used to describe unreliable statements made by eyewitnesses in courtrooms.

In the film Rashomon, a murder is described by four witnesses in contradictory ways. A person's memory, his outlook on life, perspective, physical condition, interests, and life circumstances all influence this eyewitness account.

This film and the Rashomon effect have influenced countless films throughout history. The Rashomon effect has transcended movie and become a commonly used term in psychology and law. The Rashomon effect is commonly used by judges and lawyers in the legal system when first-hand witnesses come forward with contradictory testimony.

84. Baader-Meinhoff Phenomenon

This cognitive bias is known as frequency bias or the Bader-Meinhoff phenomenon. The term was first coined in 2005 by Stanford University linguistics professor Arnold Zwicky. Zwicky concludes that the Bader-Meinhoff phenomenon is caused by two cognitive biases. The first is "selective attention bias." Here we selectively pay attention to certain things and ignore the rest. A second cognitive bias is "confirmation bias." That means we only look for things that support our ideas and ignore things that don't.

For example you are thinking of buying Tata's Nexon car. After that you start noticing its advertisements in many places. You understand that there is a lot of this vehicle on the road. It is actually a game of your brain. All these ads and this vehicle have been there before.

Religious people may interpret the Baader-Meinhoff phenomena as messages from God. Naturalists would think that this phenomenon is the universe trying to communicate with us.

85. The Pratfall Effect

People feel special affection for people who make some ridiculous mistakes in the midst of a society. That is, people who are considered highly capable by society make some small mistakes, and people feel more love for them. This effect was first studied in 1966 by social psychologist Elliott Aronson. Aronson says that people who others consider "superior" are more attractive when they make small mistakes. High people are viewed as "superhuman" by others.

Therefore, when they make a small mistake, others can see them as normal people. So people like them more. When you make a mistake you look like a raw man. People may feel that perfect people are unattainable. People have an idea that imperfect people are safe. They gain more mass.

They are seen as more likable when a person makes a mistake in society or acts strangely enough to make people laugh. People like people who make mistakes more compared to more intelligent and smart people who don't make any mistakes at all. These kinds of mistakes like spilling the tea on the body while taking a drink, stuttering, stammering etc are often added in the script of the celebrities. Many examples of this can be found in movies.

Pratfall effect experiments reveal three important social truths:

1. Being wrong is not that big of a mistake. If a person is generally considered smart and talented, making a small mistake can make them generally more socially attractive.
2. If individuals are treated as average, their mistake is more likely to affect them negatively.
3. Other factors, including gender, differentially influence the pratfall effect.

86. Zeigarnik Effect

The Zeigarnik Effect is a psychological phenomenon that describes the tendency to remember interrupted or incomplete tasks more easily than completed tasks. This phenomenon was first noticed in the early 1900s and has been confirmed by many studies.

The effect is named after the Russian psychiatrist and psychologist Bluma Wolfovna Seegarnik. While dining in a restaurant in the 1920s, Seegarnik noticed that waiters could simultaneously keep track of complex orders and people who did not pay. But Dr. Zeigarnik found that they could not recall the information about the people who had already paid the bill.

The Zeigarnik effect plays an important role in a person's mental health. Incomplete tasks, especially those with negative consequences, often lead us to frequent and stressful unnecessary thoughts. These thoughts can reduce sleep, increase anxiety, and further deplete a person's mental and emotional resources. It may even lead to misbehavior.

Conversely, the Zeigarnik effect can promote psychological well-being by motivating a person to complete tasks, develop better habits, and solve lingering problems. Successful completion of assigned tasks boosts confidence and self-esteem and gives people a sense of accomplishment. And there comes a point where mental energy is spent on less stressful events. It provides psychological well-being to a person.

If you're preparing for an exam, break up your study sessions into several sessions instead of trying to cram everything in the night before the exam. By going over and over things like this, you're more likely to remember them on test day.

If you're struggling to memorize something important, taking breaks between studies can help you remember what you've learned. Instead of repeating something over and over again, take a break after reviewing it a few times. After that, you will notice that your focus returns to the information you are learning while you focus on other things.

87. The Well-Traveled Road Effect

You are driving to a new place. Your thought is that no matter how much you travel, you are not reaching the destination. It seems like it took a long time to travel. But when you come back by the same route, you think it didn't take that long. This is a common experience for drivers.

Driving on unfamiliar roads makes you feel that everything is negative. Other vehicles, the road surface, traffic lights, bikers breaking the law all annoy you. You know it's only a short distance, but it feels like it's taking longer.

Psychologically there are many things that make this journey seem longer than it really is. The strangeness of the ways plays a key role in this. Our curiosity is sparked by the unknown. New names, landscapes and buildings attract our attention. Our focus on these novelties subtly influences our perception of how much time has passed.

But think about driving down a familiar road. It can be on your way to work, on your way to town or on your way home. You know every twist and turn there without seeing it. On these types of trips, drivers pay very little attention to the surrounding scenery. The truth is that you think this journey takes less time than it actually does. This is called the constant path effect.

This effect is caused by the way we focus. You feel that the time moves faster because you do not have to concentrate as much when you travel a familiar route. Later, when we have to think about it, we don't remember the trip very well because we don't remember the time. So we assume it was a relatively short trip.

88. Tamagotchi Effect

The Tamagotchi effect refers to our emotional attachment to machines, robots, or software robots. This tendency occurs when humans become emotionally attached to objects that do not have feelings. For example, there are times when people have feelings for their car keys or software programs they use regularly. Humans feel attached to applications that reflect certain aspects of human behavior or traits. People have an emotional attachment to machines and software programs that express knowledge, powered by artificial intelligence.

Tamagotchi is a Japanese toy released in 1996. As of 2010, over 76 million Tamagotchi have been sold worldwide. This toy is a virtual pet in the shape of an egg. It is used by people of all ages. When this toy first came out, there wasn't much criticism. But if the owner is not careful, this pet's life would end quickly. This caused emotional difficulties in people. With that, owners started taking their pets with them wherever they traveled . It has adversely affected their daily lives. As a result, many schools have banned the use of Tamagotchi. The Tamagotchi effect has already received mainstream media attention.

Benefits

Virtual 'friends' can perhaps provide us with security and confidence. This is especially beneficial for those who have difficulty communicating or interacting with others. People may rely on their virtual friends for positive encouragement or companionship.

Disadvantages

It is true that these virtual 'friends' do a lot of good for people. But people have concerns when they have to depend on it too much. Over-reliance on these digital pets can also lead to isolation from the real world. Later on it becomes difficult to distinguish between reality and fantasy. Children are especially affected by this.

89. Birthday Problem

What is the probability that two people in a small group have the same birthday? In a room of just 23 people, there is a 50-50 chance that at least two people will have the same birthday. In a room of 75 people, the probability that at least two people have the same birthday is 99.9%.

Law of truly large numbers

Have you noticed how many rare similarities you have with your spouse? The month you both were born, the day you started school, the scar on your forehead, your childhood traits, your favorite songs, and so on, these rare similarities go on. You must think that the relationship between you was nature's decision, right? The truth is that there is nothing unusual about it. In our small state millions of people live.Here there will naturally be many similarities between those living at almost the same time, in the same place,and with the same religious-social-cultural background.

Write down on a piece of paper a few characteristics that you think are unique to you. When attending a wedding reception, or in a crowd of relatives or friends, find out if anyone else has these rare characteristics that are unique to you. The fact is that even at a party of just five hundred people, there will be at least five people who share your rarity.

When large numbers exceed a threshold, they exceed our brain's counting capacity. There are many things that happen completely coincidentally in many places, but they are considered to be our own experiences. There are billions of people on this planet, billions of events, and billions of strange coincidences.

Let us look at the definition of such unusual events given by mathematician John Littlewoods .A miracle is something that has a special meaning and is likely to happen only once in a million. His mathematical conclusion was that an average person would encounter at least 10 such miracles a year.

 The odds of something resembling any dream happening to us are about one in a million. A person experiences thousands of emotions in a week. It is very easy to find some connection between these dreams and the events of his life. We find great meaning and significance in every dream. These meanings are all the result of our wishful thinking, magical thinking, and perceptual biases.

90. The Hedonic Treadmill

A person's level of happiness may rise or fall in response to happy or sad life events. But after that, the person returns to whatever his mental state was before these experiences. This phenomenon is called the hedonic treadmill.

 The process by which the effect of extremely high levels of happiness or sadness quickly fades is called hedonic adaptation. There are many different ways to understand hedonic adaptation. Let's look at some interesting examples.

People who win the lottery tend to return to their original level of happiness after the novelty of winning wears off. You might have noticed that some people become unhappy after they become financially rich and that affects their relationships too. Of course, it is true that there is great joy when you hear that you have won the lottery. After about a year after that, people begin to feel just normal happiness in their everyday lives.

The same is true for those whose bodies lose their strength in severe accidents. At first, their grief will be intense. But after a few days of habituation, people generally return to their pre-accident level of happiness. The euphoria you get when you first taste a delicious meal will never happen again.

Research shows that 50% of our level of happiness is genetic. Whereas 10% of happiness is primarily due to where we are born and to whom we are born. That means the remaining 40% is due to life circumstances.

You may feel a sense of accomplishment when you perform meaningful activities, such as volunteering for a good cause or helping a friend. These may require significant amounts of energy. When a person engages in volunteer work, because they are challenging it would not be always enjoyable for him. But they give lasting results in terms of overall happiness and inner peace. Remember that altruism actually has many benefits for both the giver and the recipient.

91. Self-Fulfilling Prophecy

A person makes a prediction and makes every effort to make that prediction come true, consciously and unconsciously. This is called a self-fulfilling prophecy. These unconscious efforts may be made by the person who made the prophecy or by the person who believed the prophecy.

There is a belief in every society that if a person firmly believes something to be true then it will be true. Often we see these firm beliefs and confidence leading them to the fruition of what they believe in. The most popular quote from the novel The Alchemist says "When you want something, all the universe conspires in helping you to achieve it"

Similar prophecies can be seen in our daily life. It can be about an event or a person's character. For those prophecies to come true it is the responsibility and necessity of the person who made the prophecy and they will take steps to do so.

For example, when you wake up in the morning, a lizard jumps on your body. 'It's a bad omen You get a thought that 'today is going to be a very bad day' . This attitude of yours may make your prediction come true. By ignoring all the good things around you and exaggerating the bad, you will make yourself feel bad that day.

And so your prediction comes true. A good example of a self-correcting prophecy is the Pygmalion effect.

The Pygmalion effect

The Pygmalion effect or Rosenthal effect is a psychological phenomenon. It has been found that higher expectations of a person in a given area lead to better performance.

For example, a teacher who believes that one of her students is very smart and will do very well academically. That teacher will definitely give more attention, encouragement and help to the child. It is not only because of the love for that student she is putting this extra effort. It is very important for the teacher that her belief and prediction are correct. Similarly, this student will also try not to break the faith and hope of the teacher. Thus favorable circumstances, encouragement, and determination help the student to live up to the expectations of his beloved teacher.

When we believe something about ourselves we are more likely to act in ways that are consistent with our beliefs. Thus we reinforce those beliefs of ours and encourage the same behavior. Similarly, when we believe something about others, we may act in ways that encourage them to confirm our assumptions. Thus our beliefs about them will be strengthened. We don't think much about these cycles when the results are positive, but when the results are negative there is a common term for these cycles - Vicious Cycles.

92. Source Monitoring Error

A memory error called "source monitoring error" occurs when we try to remember something or when we try to remember the source of something we heard before. When we remember an event, it is somewhat difficult to remember whether it actually happened or whether it was a dream or a movie. This is a processing error that is happening when our brain tries to verify whether an event was in dream or reality. People use many methods to determine the source of a memory or idea. A small processing error in our brains causes us to misinterpret the source of something.

An example of this error is when we remember a dream conversation as a real event. These errors can be caused by brain damage, memory loss, the effects of aging, depression, and high emotional stress. Cognitive biases too can cause source observation errors.

93. False Uniqueness Bias

It is a person's failure to realize the fact that there are many people around them who share the same attitudes and behaviors. Individuals think their ways and characteristics are more unusual and rare than they really are. Haven't you heard many people say that I am completely different?

The Psychology of Mind Deception

For example, a person may think that their ability in sports is something unique to them. They do not consider that there are millions of people who are equally good or more talented than them in sports. Individuals who regularly engage in physical exercise tend to underestimate the number of other people who exercise. They may also estimate that there are many people who engage in undesirable traits and behaviors (such as smoking cigarettes), or peers who behave the same way they do.

The opposite idea is the False Consensus Effect. This is a person's tendency to overestimate how much other people agree with them. Due to this effect, people think that all the other members agree with them. The reality may be quite the opposite. Due to this, the leader in a group may make many wrong decisions.

94. Blaming the Victim

It is the tendency to attribute the victim's suffering to the victim's own behaviors or characteristics rather than to a perpetrator or situational factors. Many people blame the victim in rape cases in India. People say that she was molested for wearing jeans, for going out untimely, and for going to a movie.

Why do people blame the victims?

Victim blaming often stems from a desire to see the world as a just and fair place where all people get what they deserve. This belief in a just world leads people to see the world as stable and orderly. The truth is that it is good for our survival to some extent. If people did not believe in a just world, it would have been difficult for us to pursue long-term goals, get out of bed in the morning, or commit to ourselves. People are very reluctant to give up this belief because believing in a perfectly just world is so favorable in life.

When an injustice is done to someone, it undermines people's belief that there is justice and fairness in the world. Believing that the victim deserves what actually happened to him is how people find ways to avoid this threat to their belief system. People can maintain the belief that the world is a fair place by belittling victims and blaming them for their negative outcomes.

One of the psychological benefits of victim blaming is that people have the firm belief and comfort that they will never suffer the same fate as the victim. When Hurricane Katrina hit the United States in August 2005, many residents of New Orleans were trapped inside the Superdome for days. Many blamed them for not evacuating in time despite clear weather warnings.

In reality, many people trapped in the Superdome did not have any transportation to get out of the city. They had no place to go or money to go. By blaming hurricane victims for their suffering, people are able to maintain the belief that the world is fair and just. Ultimately victim blaming allows people to maintain their own sense of control. It makes them think 'that would never have happened to me because I would have done things differently'.

The Psychology of Mind Deception

95. Polarized Thinking

A state of thinking that either everything is right or nothing is right. This Black & White thinking   is called polarized thinking. This distortion occurs when people routinely over think.

This is a state of believing that everything in your life is a success or that everything is a total failure. It means that you are stuck in polarized thinking when you think that all the people you meet are either angels or all people are evil. This type of distortion is unrealistic and often unhelpful. The truth is that reality exists somewhere between the two extremes.

When our minds play tricks to convince us of something that is actually untrue, it could prove a sick joke. If we are not careful, we may fall into it unknowingly. For example, if you fail an exam, you may think that you are a big failure at everything. The reality is that you are only one of those who have failed that exam, you are not a failure at every time and you have passed many other exams before this. This kind of black-and-white- thinking forces us to make wrong decisions.

Side effects of polarized thinking

It's okay to have polarized thoughts from time to time. No one is perfect and that is what makes us human. But this can affect and harm your relationships especially if it comes to risky life decisions.

For example, instead of reaching a middle ground around an issue, you may run away from the issue and you may never return.

Examples:
1. Quitting jobs suddenly after a heated argument with your boss / Dismissing an employee randomly or abruptly.

2. Break up with someone suddenly

3. Refrains from pursuing new friendships

96. Jumping to Conclusions

This is a phenomenon where people jump to conclusions based on insufficient information. Doing so can lead to a variety of problems.

For example, there are people who think that a person is unfriendly just because he does not smile when he talks. Here people assume things based on their past knowledge, experience, and beliefs. If people see a restaurant with faded walls, they will quickly decide that the food they are serving is bad. There will probably be good and tasty food served in that restaurant. Or if you see someone driving an expensive car, you will assume that he is rich. He could sometimes be a paid driver of that vehicle.

Mind Reading: Many people assume that they know exactly what will happen in the future. Mind reading is about thinking that you can know exactly what other people are thinking. In fact, you can only know what someone is thinking only if they openly reveal their thoughts. For example, if you say good morning to someone and they don't respond, you assume that they hate you. In Fact they might have preoccupied with something and have not heard you.

Extreme extrapolation: Here people jump to a big conclusion over a small matter. For example, after seeing some smoke coming out of a house window people assume that the house is on fire.

Over Generalization: Presuppose one small piece of knowledge or event and assume that it applies to everything. For example, assuming that only because you do not get along with someone from a certain social group, you would not get along with anyone else from that group. In some cases, this is also known as a hasty generalization or false generalization. The main reason people jump to conclusions is that our cognitive system relies on mental shortcuts (called heuristics).

Drawing conclusions this way can be problematic. Even if we don't have any evidence to support our conclusion, many mistakes are made when we make a big leap from small details to a big conclusion.

97. Correspondence Bias

 Correspondence bias is the human tendency to assume a definite picture of someone's personality based on their one time past behavior. Always remember that each person's behavior can be fully explained by his current situation. But when we see someone behaving in a certain way and tend to think - that they always behave that way it could prove detrimental. Based on their present behavior we immediately assume that they are just 'that kind of person'. We think this way even when a perfectly rational external factor motivates one's behavior. Even knowing their situation does not change our initial assessment of that person.

Examples of correspondence bias

Example one: You are dining in a restaurant. Suddenly we hear someone talking on a cell phone. The place is relatively quiet so this person's phone conversation seems very annoying. You quickly judge them. "What a bad person. Rude."

In fact, this person was going through a very bad situation. Their daughter had a problem at school. In general, this woman is not a person who talks very loudly on the phone in public. The other person could not hear what they were saying. That is why they entered this hotel and talked loudly. But we will not consider this fact. Instead of thinking about the reasons why she was talking loudly on the phone, we jump to the conclusion that she is a bad person.

Example two: You call your friend on the phone. you are desperate to talk to him. But he doesn't pick up the phone or call back. You know that he is in the middle of a divorce and is under a lot of stress. But you consider it too bad that he hasn't called you back yet.

The Malayalam movie actor Suraj Venjaramood's once narrated his experience when his brother died. After seeing his brother's dead body, when he came out of the hospital he was treated very strangely by the people outside. Some people asked him to say some joke. When he refused, people were furious,

People exhibit correspondence bias for many reasonsAs you expect people to behave in a certain way, you do not even consider the external factors that influence them. Finally, even if you are aware of the external factors and know not to blame the person, you will not be willing to change the opinion that is first formed in your mind.

98. Authority Bias

Authority bias is the tendency to blindly follow or trust the suggestions and views of a person in authority. As humans, we have evolved over millions of years as a group led by a leader. Only the leader or a group of their trusted advisors made the big decisions and the rest followed suit. As a result, humans have a deep-rooted sense of duty to follow authority. In ancient times, the roles of authority were played by kings, queens, and ministers. Today, politicians and CEOs play that role. Even experts in a profession, such as doctors, economists, and celebrities, take on the role of authority figures.

In the past not everyone had the knowledge and information to make the right decision. So the leader helped the country as a whole in taking the decision. Today the world has moved on. Every person has education and enough knowledge to make decisions.

Problems of power bias
People in positions of power may make decisions based on their instincts without thinking them through. In such cases, we obey it without question. Such opinions and decisions may have serious consequences for you and others.

Real-life examples

a. Stock markets
Every day, people follow analysts on news channels and 'experts' on websites. Many buy stocks recommended by analysts and expect good returns on their investment. Countless people have lost huge chunks of their investments by following the advice of people they considered to be authorities on the subject. We do not

understand the fact that experts cannot predict all factors that contribute to random effects. For example, no expert could have predicted the stock market crash of 2008.

b. Sports event winners

The expert panel discusses several possibilities and outcomes before the game begins. Audiences trust their word and even share it on social media. How often do such predictions come true? A lot of people who bet based on expert opinions end up losing money.

Statistics clearly show that predictions made by experts are not necessarily more accurate or better than any other layman's prediction. It's true that their experience helps you find things you cannot find. But it does not guarantee the accuracy of the results.

Here are some of the mistakes we make regularly

People believe in everything that is told by successful people. They blindly follow the advice of spiritual masters, believe everything that their manager says as true fact , and take it as sacred scripture .When celebrities, and doctors who make YouTube videos talk about medical and non-medical topics, or about everything under the sun people tend to blindly believe in it , though it may not be scientifically correct.

99. Stereotypes

Stereotypes are beliefs that certain characteristics and behaviors are common to members of a particular group. We often categorize people based on visible characteristics. For example, we make inferences about people based on their skin color, gender, age, height, religion, language, country, and many more. Stereotypes are formed in our minds based on information we receive from direct personal experience, from other people, and through the media. These stereotypes help us understand people when we have limited opportunities for meaningful interaction with people outside our own community. The media has a major role in shaping and forming stereotypes.

Benefits of stereotypes

A lot of information reaches our brains at once. The human brain has a natural tendency to categorize everything. Without an efficient way to process this information, our brains quickly tire. By classifying stimuli (e.g. experiences, objects and people) into categories, we can process our environments more efficiently. This frees up mental resources for other tasks.

Problems of stereotypes

Some stereotypes are generalizations about a group of people. For example, it is generally true that younger people have better hearing than older people. But many of our stereotypes are not necessarily true — especially if they are based on race, religion, or gender. These stereotypes can be problematic and counterproductive when interacting with others.

Arbitrariness

Stereotypes are arbitrary ways of classifying individuals. No social group is homogeneous. Stereotypes may not accurately represent the characteristics of a particular member of that group. Therefore, if a manager judges an employee only by his caste, religion, ethnicity or cultural background that could prove to be unjust.

Prejudice and discrimination

 Prejudice refers to our feelings or attitudes about a group and its members. Prejudice is usually associated with stereotypes. We think our judgments about others are true.

Discrimination refers to the different (usually unfair or negative) treatment of individuals belonging to a particular social group. For example, people may be overlooked or treated with hostility by others due to this prejudice in promotion or hiring.

100. Narrative Bias

Narrative bias forces us to see events with logical chains of multiple causes and effects as mere stories. Stories help us understand the world. However, if we are not aware of narrative bias, we can lead ourselves to believe that we understand the world more than we actually do.

 We, humans, are generally not good at objectively assessing the uncertainty that occurs in our lives. Our brains have a universal tendency to find meaning and patterns in all areas of life. It is through this evolutionarily acquired program that we better understand the world around us and, to some extent, control it.

Random events cannot explain why certain things happen. We have the urge to explain everything. When an unpredictable event occurs, people come up with simple and fitting explanatory stories. Our minds find happiness by treating the world as simple, predictable, and agreeable to us. This pattern-seeking tendency is called narrative bias. It is very important to recognize this mental bias because the events that happen around us do not happen in any exact order.

See the gambler's fallacy. When a coin is tossed and heads come up five times in a row, people tend to believe that the next flip is more likely to come up with tails than heads. However, any flip has an equal chance of coming up heads or tails. Coins have no memory. That is, the coin does not 'know' what the previous results were. Therefore, it is possible to get heads ten times or tails ten times.

Based on the present years' flood we could not be able to tell whether there will be a flood next year. But our intuitive mind tells us that just because there was a flood this year, there is less chance of a flood next year. Our brains cannot understand the nature of randomness.

The Psychology of Mind Deception

It is not always clear whether our success in a job is due to some act of our own doing or it happens by chance or not. But we make up stories in our favor. Even a clock that has stopped running right twice a day. The world is complicated and it tricks us. Much of what happens to us (eg, our career success, our life choices) are the result of many random factors rather than the result of preparation and hard work.

101. Reverse Halo Effect

We don't accept any qualities from a person or an organization that we do not like, or that we hate. The human brain does not bother to analyze each thing and the characteristics of individuals on the basis of an objective and rational manner. We would not waste our emotional energy to analyze a matter statistically or logically and reach a decision. Here, decisions are made by emotions over thoughts.

You will never like the products or actions of people, organizations, or people we dislike, no matter how good they are. Your mind will find reasons to explain why you hate them.

This is the main reason why the gap between individuals, movements, and countries is so endless, and the issues last without any solution and we believe that no consensus is possible. This is the reason why Muslims in Pakistan believe that the destruction of the World Trade Organization headquarters was done by Jews or it was done by Hindus.

In 1920, psychologist Edward Thorndike observed a phenomenon which he called the "reverse halo effect" in his article titled "Persistent Error in Psychological Ratings." To study this effect, he requested commanding officers to evaluate soldiers based on specific attributes such as intelligence, leadership, character, and creativity. However, he noticed that these officers were primarily basing their evaluations on the soldiers' physical appearance rather than their actual abilities.

As we have seen earlier in this book the term "halo effect" was initially coined by psychologist Edward L. Thorndike to describe a cognitive bias in which the impression of a person in one area carries over to another area. For example, if someone is seen as physically attractive, they might be rated more favorably in other areas like intelligence or character, even if those ratings aren't necessarily warranted.

However, in the case of the "reverse halo effect," the opposite occurs. Rather than a positive attribute influencing a person's rating in other areas, a negative attribute, in this case, the soldier's physical appearance, influences their ratings in all other areas.

****

The Psychology of Mind Deception

Bibliography:

1. Ariely, Dan. (2008). Predictably Irrational: The Hidden Forces That Shape Our Decisions (HarperCollins).

2. Thinking, Fast and Slow" by Daniel Kahneman

3. The Art of Thinking Clearly" by Rolf Dobelli

4. Mistakes Were Made (But Not by Me): Why We Justify Foolish Beliefs, Bad Decisions, and Hurtful Acts" by Carol Tavris and Elliot Aronson

5. The Psychology of Judgment and Decision Making" by Scott Plous

6. The Halo Effect: ... and the Eight Other Business Delusions That Deceive Managers" by Phil Rosenzweig

7. The Invisible Gorilla: How Our Intuitions Deceive Us" by Christopher Chabris and Daniel Simons

8. Nudge: Improving Decisions About Health, Wealth, and Happiness" by Richard Thaler and Cass Sunstein

9. "You Are Not So Smart: Why You Have Too Many Friends on Facebook, Why Your Memory Is Mostly Fiction, and 46 Other Ways You're Deluding Yourself" by David McRaney

10. "The Skeptic's Guide to the Universe: How to Know What's Really Real in a World Increasingly Full of Fake" by Steven Novella, Bob Novella, Jay Novella, Cara Santa Maria, and Evan Bernstein

11. Dawes, Robyn M. Everyday Irrationality: How Pseudo-Scientists, Lunatics, and the Rest of Us Systematically Fail to Think Rationally (Westview Press 2003).

12. Gardner, Martin. Fads and Fallacies in the Name of Science (New York: Dover Publications, Inc., 1957),

13. Gardner, Martin. Science: Good, Bad and Bogus (Buffalo, N.Y.: Prometheus Books, 1981),

14. Gilovich, Thomas. How We Know What Isn't' So: The Fallibility of Human Reason in Everyday Life (New York: The Free Press, 1993).

15. Kahneman, Daniel. Paul Slovic, and Amos Tversky. eds. 1982. Judgment Under Uncertainty: Heuristics and Biases Cambridge University Press.

16. Levine, Robert. 2003. The Power of Persuasion - How We're Bought and Sold. John Wiley & Sons.

The Psychology of Mind Deception

17. Sagan, Carl. The Demon-Haunted World - Science as a Candle in the Dark (New York: Random House, 1995).

18. Sternberg, Robert J. ed. Why Smart people Can Be So Stupid. (Yale University Press 2002).

19. Sutherland, Stuart. (2007). Irrationality. 2rev edition (Pinter & Martin Ltd).

20. Fabrigar, L. R., & Krosnick, J. A. (1995). Attitude importance and the false consensus effect. Personality and Social Psychology Bulletin, 21, 468-479.

21. Lawson, R. (2006). The science of Psychology: Failures understand how everyday objects work. Memory &Cognition, 34, 1667-1675.

22. Baron, J. (2000). Thinking and deciding (3d. edition). New York: Cambridge University Press. ISBN 0-521-65030-5

23. Bishop, Michael A & Trout, J.D. (2004). Epistemology and the Psychology of Human Judgment. New York: Oxford University Press. ISBN 0-19-516229-3

24. Gilovich, T. (1993). How We Know What Isn't So: The Fallibility of Human Reason in Everyday Life. New York: The Free Press. ISBN 0-02-911706-2

25. Gilovich, T., Griffin D. & Kahneman, D. (Eds.). (2002). Heuristics and biases: The psychology of intuitive judgment. Cambridge, UK: Cambridge University Press. ISBN 0-521-79679-2

26. Kahneman, Daniel, Jack L. Knetsch, and Richard H. Thaler. (1991). "Anomalies: The Endowment Effect, Loss Aversion, and Status Quo Bias." The Journal of Economic Perspectives 5(1):193-206.

27. Haselton, M. G. & Buss, D. M. (2003). Biases in Social Judgment: Design Flaws or Design Features? In J. Forgas, K. Williams, & B. von Hippel (Eds.) Responding to the Social World: Implicit and Explicit Processes in Social Judgments and Decisions. New York, NY: Cambridge.

28. https://effectiviology.com/

29. https://boycewire.com/

30. https://www.medicalnewstoday.com/

31. https://www.ifioque.com/social-psychology/representative-heuristic